American Heart Association®

Fighting Heart Disease and Stroke

low-fat & luscious
desserts

cakes, cookies, pies, and other temptations

American Heart
Association.

Fighting Heart Disease and Stroke

low-fat & luscious
desserts

cakes, cookies, pies, and other temptations

American Heart Association
Clarkson Potter/Publishers

New York   W

Your contribution to the American Heart Association supports research that helps make publications like this possible. For more information, call 1-800-AHA-USA1 (1-800-242-8721) or contact us online at www.americanheart.org.

Published by Clarkson Potter/Publishers, New York, New York. Member of the Crown Publishing Group.

Random House, Inc. New York, Toronto, London, Sydney, Auckland
www.randomhouse.com

CLARKSON N. POTTER is a trademark and POTTER and colophon are registered trademarks of Random House, Inc.

Printed in the United States of America

Design by Jan Derevjanik

Library of Congress Cataloging-in-Publication Data
American Heart Association low-fat & luscious desserts.
    Includes index.
    1. Low-fat diet—Recipes. 2. Desserts. I. Title: American Heart Association low-fat and luscious desserts. II. Title: Low-fat & luscious desserts. III. American Heart Association.
RM237.7.A438   2000
641.5'638—dc21   00-035698

ISBN 0-8129-3336-2

10 9 8 7 6 5 4 3 2 1

First Edition

Front cover: Mixed Berry Tart with Apricot Glaze (page 64)

acknowledgments

American Heart Association Director, Consumer Publications: Jane Anneken Ruehl

American Heart Association Senior Editor: Janice Roth Moss

American Heart Association Science Editor: Ann Melugin Williams

American Heart Association Science Consultant: Terry Bazzarre, Ph.D.

American Heart Association Editorial Coordinator: Marquel Dibrell Huebotter

American Heart Association Editorial Assistant: Roberta Westcott Sullivan

Recipe Developers: Carol Ritchie
Nancy S. Hughes
Beatrice Ojakangas
George Geary
Ruth Mossok Johnston
Robin Vitetta-Miller
Christy Rost
Dede Wilson
Karen Levin
Linda Foley Woodrum

Writer: Pat Harmon Naegele

Nutrient Analyses: Hancock Nutrition Analysis

Clarkson Potter Executive Editor: Elizabeth Rapoport

Photographer: Ben Fink

Assistant to Photographer: Holly McDade

Food Stylist: Kevin Crafts

Assistant to Food Stylist: Sharon Core

contents

preface

When you were a kid, how did you show that you loved your best friend? By sharing that chocolate brownie from your lunch box, of course! It's no different today. When you celebrate a birthday . . . when it's some other special occasion . . . when guests come over for dinner, you still share dessert. Many of us consider sharing good food—including good desserts—to be a sign of friendship and camaraderie. At the American Heart Association, we know that although desserts are a small part of a heart-healthy diet, they're a large part of celebrating life.

This cookbook is proof that you can indulge in satisfying desserts—and still keep your heart healthy and your waistline trim. In fact, some desserts even supply nutrients your body needs. Take a fruit-based dessert, such as our Tropical Fruit Pie (page 60). This light and lively dessert provides vitamins A and C, potassium, and beta carotene. If you choose a dessert that's based on fat-free or low-fat dairy products, such as our Cheesecake with Fresh Berry Sauce (page 26), you get calcium, protein, and other nutrients.

The key to fitting desserts into a healthful eating plan is moderation. We're not suggesting dessert with every meal. Far from it. But when you *do* decide to have a sweet treat, make it one of ours. You'll find that they're heavy on taste but light on fat, especially saturated fat, and cholesterol.

Impossible? Look again! We've packed this cookbook with more than one hundred of the most mouthwatering desserts on the planet. Yet each of them fits easily into a healthful eating plan. From our rich Chocolate Walnut Brownies (page 92) to the tantalizing Mocha Fudge Angel Pie (page 94), you'll find recipes to make your taste buds smile. One bite of our Banana Bonanza Cake (page 15) will show that you don't have to splurge on fats, cholesterol, and calories to enjoy a truly delectable dessert.

When the tantalizing aroma of our Apple Snack Cake (page 23) lures your family into the kitchen, you can feel good about offering this wholesome treat. As for guests, well, you may never get rid of them! Our scene-stealing Maui Cheesecake (page 25) makes an unforgettable four-star presentation. Yet our recipes are much lower in saturated fat and cholesterol than such splendid desserts usually are. Most are also lower in calories.

How did we do it? We charged some outstanding chefs with creating wonderful desserts that have your heart and health in mind. And did they meet the challenge! So go ahead. Give in to temptation.

introduction

The American Heart Association has created a desserts-only cookbook! That means we can eat dessert at every meal, right?

Nice try.

It's tempting to look at this cookbook and go wild, but cooler and healthier heads must prevail. The American Heart Association diet (see Appendix A) will show you that the foundation for wholesome, heart-smart eating is vegetables, fruits, whole grains, legumes, protein, and fat-free or low-fat dairy products. Sweets fit in only as an *occasional* treat. But, oh, what a treat.

down-to-earth talk about out-of-this-world desserts

Some people may think that the term "nutritious desserts" is an oxymoron. At the American Heart Association we say, "It's possible!" If your dessert contains fruit, for example, it includes vitamins, minerals, and fiber.

Our Farmer's Market Snack Cake (page 24) is positively blissful, and it contains nutrients from carrots, zucchini, and whole grains. Our tempting Mixed Berry Tart with Apricot Glaze (page 64), tangy Lime Fool with Raspberries and Kiwifruit (page 105), and totally luscious Triple-Berry, Triple-Citrus Summer Pudding (page 114) will bring tears of joy to your eyes, yet the recipes are packed with vitamin C. From Wine-Poached Pears with Vanilla Sauce (page 124) and Berries Brûlée (page 126) to Roasted Fresh Peaches with Pistachio Stuffing (page 129), you'll find plenty of nutrition on these pages. As long as you keep one eye on the total amount of fat, saturated fat, and calories you eat, you can enjoy adding these desserts to your menu.

zen and the art of desserts

Desserts should not only be indulgent and satisfying, they should complement the meal. It's a matter of balance. For example, let's say you're serving a hot-and-spicy entrée. You may want to choose a soothing frozen dessert, such as Sunset Sorbet (page 134) or Zinfandel Granita (page 135), to add another element to the meal. When you serve a simple grilled chicken breast, brown rice pilaf, and steamed broccoli, that's a good time to consider a fancier, rich-tasting dessert—our Chocolate Mini-Soufflés (page 98), for instance. In the winter, when heartier meals such as pot roast and chili are popular, try a light dessert. Ginger Nut Cookies (page 42) or Skillet Cherry Crumble (page 70) would be perfect.

The key is to combine elements such as textures (smooth, crunchy, crumbly) and tastes (tart, sweet, mild) in a way that pleases your senses.

cool desserts from hot chefs

For this cookbook, we pulled together the *crème de la crème*—four-star pastry chefs, a former bakery owner, cookbook authors, and cooking teachers so you can treat yourself to delightful, delicious desserts that are consistent with American Heart Association guidelines for reducing the saturated fat and cholesterol in your diet. We'd like to tell you a little about the experts who developed the truly indulgent desserts that await you.

the dream team

When it's time to pull out all the stops for a party and tickle your guests—and their taste buds—with a dessert that's so different they'll be talking about it for days, take a look at our "Hamburger" Cake (page 12). A creation from Carol Ritchie, who delights audiences with her TV cooking shows, cooking classes, and seminars, it is a unique dessert that features two kinds of cake for the "meat" and the "bun," plus fruit for the "condiments." Also try Green Tea and Banana Frozen Yogurt in Crispy Baskets (page 138) from the same recipe developer. Served with juicy tangelo slices in individual baskets made of egg roll wrappers, it's a creamy, cooling confection.

Then feast your senses on creamy Tiramisù (page 106), reinvented for us by Nancy S. Hughes, the author of seven low-fat, low-calorie cookbooks and coauthor of eight other cookbooks. "This dessert is heaven," says the chef, who also develops recipes for major healthful cooking and lifestyle magazines. "Just leave it in the fridge overnight so the flavors mix into a rich, mellow dessert. And it has just a fraction of the fat and calories of traditional tiramisù."

When you taste Pecan-Pie Cookies (page 32), you're going to wonder who could make something so low fat taste so fantastic. The answer is George Geary, who was pastry chef for Walt Disney Company for seven years and has taught cooking classes at more than seventy schools and culinary stores in thirty-four states.

Beatrice Ojakangas, a former food editor for *Sunset Magazine,* has written twenty-two luscious cookbooks. Want a sample of her work? Sink your teeth into Apple Cappuccino Cake (page 21), a dessert that you can also enjoy at breakfast. And when it comes to light and dreamy, you won't soon forget her Coconut Flans with Dark Chocolate Sauce (page 112).

Food consultant, cookbook author, and newspaper columnist Ruth Mossok Johnston treated us to her creative genius when she developed Layered Strawberry Meringue Cake (page 4). It's a melt-in-your-mouth concoction of meringue, strawberries, and whipped topping—light and perfect for summertime.

A TV spokesperson who writes food columns for seven popular magazines, Robin Vitetta-Miller created one of our favorite recipes, Super Chocolaty Cake with whipped vanilla icing (page 78). Rich and creamy but amazingly low in fat, it looks picture-perfect when topped with fresh fruit.

magnificent obsessions

One of the prettiest desserts in this cookbook, Double-Chocolate Valentine Cake (page 82), comes from Christy Rost, a talented television chef who gives seminars on cooking and entertaining at major department stores all over the country. The heart-shaped cake with rich-tasting chocolate icing and confectioners' sugar glaze is dense and satisfying.

Another recipe developer, Dede Wilson, is a former bakery owner and pastry chef. She now is a cookbook author and cooking teacher. Her Deep, Dark Chocolate Pudding Cake (page 84) is so sensuous and opulent, you won't believe it's low in fat.

Karen Levin, a longtime food consultant and cookbook author, created a warm-weather treat that's a flavor explosion. Called Tropical Bombe (page 136), it's vibrantly colored and refreshing. Best of all, it's a no-cook dessert that won't heat up the kitchen.

A former test kitchen home economist for *Better Homes and Gardens* and assistant food editor of several of its books, Linda Foley Woodrum is an R.T. French Tastemaker award winner. One forkful of her Cheesecake with Fresh Berry Sauce (page 26) and you'll taste why.

how to use the
nutrient analyses

To help you fit dessert into a healthful diet, we've provided a nutrient analysis with each recipe in this cookbook. The analysis tells you the number of calories and the amount of protein, carbohydrate, total fat, saturated fat, polyunsaturated fat, monounsaturated fat, cholesterol, and sodium in each serving.

Armed with this information, you can easily decide how a particular dessert fits into your eating plan. If you've been extremely light on calories, you can happily splurge on any of our great desserts with no ill effects. If you need to reduce your saturated fat and cholesterol intake, you can still treat yourself to one of the delicious desserts we offer. Just look for one with very little saturated fat and low cholesterol.

While you're reading, keep these facts in mind:

❖ Single Servings. We tell you how many servings a recipe makes, and each analysis is based on a single serving. If you eat more—or less—than that amount, adjust the numbers accordingly for calories, saturated fat, and the other categories analyzed.

❖ Optional Ingredients. We did *not* include optional ingredients in the analyses. If you use them, you need to count them if they add saturated fat, cholesterol, or any other nutrient you're concerned about. The desserts are fabulous whether you include the options or leave them out.

❖ Average Amount. We analyzed any ingredient with a range, such as ½ to ¾ cup sugar, at the average amount.

❖ First Option. A recipe may list two or more ingredient options, such as 1 cup nonfat or low-fat yogurt. If it does, we used the first one in the nutrient analysis.

❖ Exact Amounts. We analyzed only the specific amounts of the ingredients listed in the recipe—not the amounts sometimes shown in parentheses. The amounts in parentheses are just guidelines to help you know how much to buy or to remove from the refrigerator, freezer, or pantry. For example, if a recipe calls for "3 tablespoons lime juice (2 limes)," we analyzed the 3 tablespoons of juice, not the 2 limes. (We usually don't list the quantity in parentheses if you'll need only one, or part of one, of the item.)

❖ Totaling the Fat. The values of saturated, monounsaturated, and polyunsaturated fats may not add up to the amount of total fat listed for the recipe. That's because the total fat includes other fatty substances not reflected in the analysis. Also, we rounded all values to the nearest whole number.

❖ Acceptable Margarine. In the analyses, we used corn oil margarine. You can use any margarine that lists liquid vegetable oil as the first ingredient and contains no more than 2 grams of saturated fat per tablespoon. Unless a recipe states otherwise, use stick margarine.

❖ Acceptable Oil. When a recipe calls for acceptable vegetable oil, we used corn oil. You can also use canola, safflower, soybean, and sunflower oil.

❖ Mix and Match. If you make creative substitutions that won't affect the recipe's nutritional analysis, you can still use that analysis. Replacing nutmeg with cinnamon and dark brown sugar with light brown are examples.

❖ Grand Garnishes. Presentation is part of a dessert's pizzazz. You can go as wild with garnishes as we did in the color photographs you'll find on these pages. Just remember: If you eat the garnishes, be sure to count any calories, fat, cholesterol, or sodium they contain.

❖ On the Alert. The United States Department of Agriculture (USDA) says that there's no difference in the nutritional values of the same food, whether fresh, frozen, or canned. However, with frozen and canned foods, you'll need to be alert to added ingredients, such as sugar, that could change the analysis and the taste. If the recipe calls for, and so was analyzed with, fresh raspberries but you use raspberries frozen in syrup, you'll consume more calories than the analysis lists.

❖ Abbreviations. You'll find gram abbreviated as "g" and milligram as "mg."

the well-stocked pantry

You'll find that you can quickly and easily pull together many of these desserts from ingredients you probably have; the key is keeping a well-stocked kitchen. Here's a guide to many of the shelf-stable, refrigerated, and frozen foods and the products used in these recipes. Hardly anyone will want to keep all these items on hand. Once you stock your kitchen with the basics you're likely to use, however, you can simplify your shopping list. You'll need to buy only the fresh or specialty ingredients a given recipe calls for. You'll find most of these items in your local grocery store; for others you'll want to visit a health food store or specialty cooking store.

SPICES, FLAVORINGS, AND SEASONINGS

- Chocolate, unsweetened chocolate squares
- Chocolate, reduced-fat semi-sweet chips and unsweetened chips
- Cinnamon, ground and stick
- Cocoa powder, unsweetened, and Dutch process, unsweetened
- Coffee, instant granules
- Extracts/flavorings (vanilla; almond; rum; coconut; peppermint; and vanilla, butter, and nut)
- Ginger, crystallized and ground
- Gingerroot
- Liqueurs (almond, black currant, chocolate, coffee, and orange)
- Mace
- Nutmeg, ground and whole
- Vinegar, white

FOR THE REFRIGERATOR

- Eggs
- Egg substitute
- Lemon juice, bottled
- Margarine sticks, acceptable or light
- Margarine tubs, fat free or light

FOR THE FREEZER

- Berries (blueberries, raspberries, and strawberries)
- Coconut, unsweetened, flaked and shredded
- Frozen whipped topping, fat free or light
- Phyllo dough
- Piecrusts, low-fat, frozen, unbaked

MISCELLANEOUS

- Aluminum foil
- Applesauce, unsweetened
- Baking powder
- Baking soda
- Cherry pie filling, canned
- Condensed milk, fat-free regular and fat-free sweetened
- Cooking parchment
- Cornstarch
- Corn syrup, dark and light
- Cream of tartar
- Evaporated milk, fat free
- Flour, cake and all-purpose
- Gelatin, unflavored
- Gingersnap cookies, reduced fat
- Graham crackers, low fat
- Plastic wrap
- Powdered egg whites
- Pudding mix, fat free
- Pumpkin, canned
- Pumpkin pie filling, canned
- Sugar (granulated, light brown, dark brown, and confectioners')
- Toothpicks, wooden
- Vanilla wafers, reduced fat
- Vegetable oil (canola, corn, safflower, soybean, or sunflower)
- Vegetable oil spray, regular and butter flavor
- Wax paper
- Whipped topping mix, powdered

basic equipment

You don't need a four-star kitchen to turn out great desserts. Saucepans, (small, medium, and large), mixing bowls (small, medium, and large), knives, cutting boards, measuring cups (dry and liquid), measuring spoons, whisks, and rubber scrapers are must-haves. In addition to a food processor or blender, you'll also need an electric mixer; a wand blender comes in handy for many small blending jobs. Here's some other basic equipment you'll want to consider:

❖ 8- and 9-inch baking pans

❖ 8- and 9-inch cake pans

❖ 9-inch pie pan

❖ baking sheets, flat and rimmed (2 of each)

❖ 13 × 9 × 2-inch baking pan

❖ 11 × 7 × 1½-inch sheet cake pan

❖ 9 × 5-inch loaf pan

❖ cupcake tins

❖ cooling racks

❖ 3- to 4- and 5- to 6-ounce ramekins or custard cups (6 or 8 of each size)

❖ 1½- to 2-quart glass bowls (good for beating egg whites and for trifle)

❖ 6-cup ring mold

❖ 9-inch springform pan

❖ double boiler

❖ pastry blender

❖ zester or food rasp

❖ candy thermometer or instant-read thermometer

Nonstick cookware helps you trim down the fat in your baking and makes cleanup a snap.

The more you cook, the more your appetite for kitchen equipment is likely to grow. You may find yourself slipping more decorative molds, pastry bags with tips, pie weights, and other specialized items into your shopping cart.

Happy hunting!

how to adapt your
favorite dessert recipes

When it comes to creating luscious desserts, most people think "fattening." This cookbook will show that you can have wonderful desserts, yet still limit your fat intake.

With the recipes in this book, we've clearly specified the ingredients you'll need to use to keep the dessert delicious without jeopardizing your cardiovascular system. But what if you want to bake your Aunt Martha's famous pound cake? Simple. You make some heart-smart substitutions and follow some tips we'll tell you about below.

For example, when a recipe calls for butter and cream, choose acceptable margarine (fat-free or light, liquid or tub if possible) and fat-free evaporated milk. You'll find that the substitutions make a big difference in the bottom line. One tablespoon of butter, for example, contains about 11 grams of fat. This includes more than 7 grams of saturated fat and 31 milligrams of cholesterol. Margarine, on the other hand, also contains about 11 grams of fat, but less than 2 grams are saturated and there's *no* cholesterol. The end result? You get the same moistness, density, and flavor, but without all the saturated fat and cholesterol.

Check the chart on page xviii for an easy-to-follow list of substitutions you can make with easy-to-find ingredients.

fat-fighting cooking tips

You're probably already using some of the following simple tips. Others may offer new ideas to make it easier for you to enjoy guilt-free treats.

NUTS

In most instances, you can cut the amount of nuts a recipe calls for by one fourth to one half. Substitute other foods with crunchy textures, such as crisp rice cereal or nugget-type cereal, for what you removed. This idea works particularly well with nonbaked goods, such as toppings for frozen yogurt.

Chopping the nuts into small pieces is another way to stretch their taste and texture.

Toasting the nuts also brings out their flavor. Preheat the oven to 350°F. Put the nuts on a baking pan, and dry-roast them until they're light brown, about 10 minutes, stirring them halfway through. You can toast them under the broiler for 2 to 3 minutes if you prefer. Keep a close watch, though, because they'll burn quickly.

WHEN YOUR RECIPE CALLS FOR . . .	USE . . .
Butter	Margarine (look for one that lists liquid vegetable oil as the first ingredient and contains no more than 2 grams of saturated fat per tablespoon).
Cream	Fat-free evaporated milk or fat-free liquid nondairy creamer.
Whole milk	Fat-free milk or fat-free or low-fat buttermilk.
Whipped cream	Frozen fat-free or light whipped topping.
Sweetened condensed milk	Fat-free sweetened condensed milk.
Regular sour cream	Nonfat or light sour cream.
Regular yogurt	Fat-free or low-fat yogurt.
Whole-milk cream cheese	Fat-free or reduced-fat cream cheese.
Ice cream	Nonfat or low-fat frozen yogurt, ice milk, or sherbet.
Whole eggs	Egg whites (substitute two egg whites for each whole egg) or egg substitute. For baked goods, beat the whites until foamy for a fluffier product.
Baking chocolate	Unsweetened cocoa powder. (In some recipes, you'll need to mix it with oil or margarine to substitute for chocolate.)

FRUITS AND VEGGIES

Want a super-moist cake without lots of fat? Use baby food prunes in place of some (or all) of the fat in chocolate desserts and unsweetened applesauce in other desserts. You'll never know the fat is missing!

For extra moisture—and nutrients—in some baked goods, you can add pureed bananas, shredded zucchini, shredded carrots, apple or other fruit butter, or canned pumpkin.

SWEET AND SPICY

When you're cutting fat in a recipe, increase the amount of flavoring you use. For example, add sweet spices, such as cinnamon, nutmeg, or cardamom, or use one and one-half times the amount of spice called for. Try doubling the amount of vanilla, or use half again as much citrus zest or almond extract as the recipe specifies. (If your recipe calls for vanilla extract, try a real vanilla bean instead. Just scrape out the seeds and add them to the recipe. Vanilla beans are more expensive than the extract, but the flavor difference is worth the price difference.)

Use less coconut than a recipe calls for (coconut is high in saturated fat), and add some coconut extract instead.

In some recipes, especially with fruit, a touch of fresh mint adds a blast of flavor.

CHOCOLATY-ER CHOCOLATE

To intensify the rich flavor of chocolate desserts, add $\frac{1}{2}$ to 1 teaspoon of instant coffee granules to the recipe.

BAKING BASICS

Measuring flour accurately is especially important in low-fat baking. Be sure to spoon the flour into the measuring cup, then level the flour with a knife.

To prevent low-fat baked goods from being tough, don't overmix batters and doughs.

MERINGUE SHELLS

Instead of a high-fat piecrust, try a meringue shell. The eggs will separate best when they are cold, but they whip best at room temperature. Separate the cold eggs carefully, putting the whites in a glass or metal mixing bowl. Be sure the bowl and beaters are absolutely clean. Even the tiniest bit of grease or egg yolk will keep the whites from whipping into peaks.

recipes

Layered Strawberry Meringue Cake

Upside-Down and Right-Side-Up Cake

Coconut-Pineapple Layer Cake

Carrot Cake with Lemony Cream Cheese Icing

Triple-Layer Sponge Cake with Lemon Cream Filling

"Hamburger" Cake

Banana Cake with Chocolate Pudding Topping

Banana Bonanza Cake

Almond Torte with Chocolate Ganache

Pumpkin Spice Cake with White Chocolate Icing

Pecan Shortcake with Peach Melba Sauce

Apple Cappuccino Cake

Apple Cinnamon Cake

Apple Snack Cake

Farmer's Market Snack Cake

Maui Cheesecake

Cheesecake with Fresh Berry Sauce

Boston Cream Cupcakes

great
cakes

layered strawberry meringue cake

SERVES 8

Elegant and easy—the perfect combination. You can prepare the components ahead of time, then assemble the dessert just before serving so the meringue layers don't get soggy.

meringue

Whites of 3 large eggs, room temperature
¾ cup sugar
1 teaspoon cornstarch
1 teaspoon fresh lemon juice

sauce

1 pint fresh strawberries, hulled and chopped (about 2 cups)
¼ to ½ cup sugar
½ cup water

1 tablespoon grated lemon zest
2 tablespoons fresh lemon juice
1 teaspoon cornstarch
2 tablespoons water

filling

1 pint fresh strawberries, hulled and chopped (about 2 cups)
6 ounces frozen fat-free or light whipped topping, thawed (about 2 cups)

❖

Whole fresh strawberries (optional)

Preheat oven to 200°F. Line two baking sheets with cooking parchment. With a thin marker, draw three 4½ × 9-inch rectangles on parchment, then flip parchment over (drawn lines will show through). Set aside.

For meringue layers, in a large mixing bowl, beat egg whites with an electric mixer on high until very stiff, glossy peaks form. (Peaks shouldn't fold over when beater is lifted.)

Add sugar, 1 to 2 tablespoons at a time, beating after each addition. (Meringue shouldn't feel gritty when rubbed between fingers.)

Add cornstarch and lemon juice; beat to mix in. Using a pastry bag with a small tip, make a border for each rectangle by piping meringue along the lines drawn with marker. Using a rubber scraper, divide meringue evenly and fill in each rectangular outline, making three rather flat rectangles; smooth each top.

Bake for 20 minutes. Increase heat to 275°F; bake for 40 minutes, or until meringue is dry and barely beige. Turn off oven and leave meringues in oven until cool (this prevents cracking). Meringues can be made up to one day ahead, covered with plastic wrap to keep out moisture, and stored at room temperature.

Calories 180
Protein 2 g
Carbohydrates 42 g
Fiber 2 g
Total Fat 0 g
  Saturated 0 g
  Polyunsaturated 0 g
  Monounsaturated 0 g
Cholesterol 0 mg
Sodium 34 mg

For sauce, in a medium, heavy saucepan, combine strawberries, sugar, ½ cup water, lemon zest, and lemon juice. Cook over medium-high heat for about 6 minutes, stirring occasionally and mashing strawberries with a wand mixer or back of a large spoon.

Put cornstarch in a small cup. Add remaining 2 tablespoons water, stirring to dissolve; stir into strawberries. Increase heat to high and bring to a boil. Reduce heat to medium; cook until mixture is thickened and cornstarch no longer appears cloudy, about 6 minutes, stirring occasionally. Let cool to room temperature, about 25 minutes. Sauce can be made up to two days in advance and refrigerated in a covered container.

For filling, in a medium bowl, gently combine strawberries and whipped topping.

To assemble, carefully remove one meringue rectangle from cooking parchment and place on a cutting board. Spread half the strawberry filling mixture over it. Repeat, ending with last meringue layer. Spoon 2 tablespoons strawberry sauce onto each of eight dessert plates. With a serrated knife, gently cut meringue cake into 8 slices. Using a spatula, carefully lift each slice and lay it on strawberry sauce. Garnish with whole strawberries. Serve immediately.

> COOK'S TIP: A wand mixer is ideal for pureeing the strawberry sauce. Try the sauce on waffles, over yogurt, or on angel food cake.

upside-down and right-side-up cake

It may be hard to choose which side of this cake to present to your guests. One side has caramelized pineapple, and the other a crunchy streusel topping. A bonus is the moist banana-flavored cake in the center of all that goodness.

Vegetable oil spray

upside-down ingredients
- 1 tablespoon light corn syrup
- 1/3 to 1/2 cup firmly packed light or dark brown sugar
- 1 8-ounce can pineapple slices in their own juice, drained and cut in half crosswise
- 6 stemless maraschino cherries, halved

cake
- 1 1/4 cups all-purpose flour
- 3/4 cup sugar
- 1 teaspoon baking powder
- 1/2 teaspoon baking soda
- 1/2 cup fat-free or low-fat buttermilk
- 1/2 cup mashed banana
- Egg substitute equivalent to 1 egg, or 1 large egg
- 1 tablespoon acceptable vegetable oil

right-side-up ingredients
- 1/2 cup quick-cooking oatmeal, uncooked
- 2 tablespoons chopped pecans
- 2 tablespoons light or dark brown sugar
- 2 tablespoons light stick margarine, softened
- 1/2 teaspoon ground cinnamon

Preheat oven to 350°F. Spray a 9-inch nonstick cake pan with vegetable oil spray.

For upside-down layer, drizzle corn syrup over bottom of pan; sprinkle with brown sugar.

Decoratively arrange pineapple slices on brown sugar; place cherries cut side up among pineapple segments.

For cake, in a large bowl, combine flour, sugar, baking powder, and baking soda.

Stir in remaining cake ingredients just until combined (mixture will be slightly lumpy). Pour over pineapple.

In a small bowl, combine right-side-up ingredients. Sprinkle over batter.

Bake for 35 to 40 minutes, or until a toothpick inserted in center comes out clean. Invert cake onto a serving platter and let cool for 30 minutes. Serve either side up.

COOK'S TIP ON MEASURING FLOUR: For the most accurate measurement, begin by lightly stirring the flour. Next, spoon it into the measuring cup, heaping the flour. With a knifeblade or other straightedge, level the flour.

Calories 248
Protein 4 g
Carbohydrates 51 g
Fiber 1 g
Total Fat 4 g
  Saturated 1 g
  Polyunsaturated 2 g
  Monounsaturated 1 g
Cholesterol 0 mg
Sodium 160 mg

low-fat & luscious desserts

coconut-pineapple layer cake

SERVES 12

A luscious, airy, coconut-flavored cake with layers of whipped topping and sweet pineapple—and not a drop of oil!

Vegetable oil spray
Flour for dusting cake pans
1 18.5-ounce reduced-fat white cake mix
1¼ cups water
Whites of 3 large eggs
1 teaspoon coconut extract

2 20-ounce cans crushed pineapple in its own juice, undrained
1 tablespoon cornstarch
12 ounces frozen fat-free or light whipped topping, thawed (about 4½ cups)

Preheat oven to 350°F. Spray two 9-inch round cake pans with vegetable oil spray. Dust lightly with flour; shake excess flour from pans. Set pans aside.

In a medium mixing bowl, combine cake mix, water, egg whites, and coconut extract; mix using package directions. Divide evenly between two pans.

Bake for about 35 minutes, or until a toothpick inserted in center comes out clean. Let stand on cooling racks for 15 minutes. Invert cakes onto racks, remove pans, and let cakes cool completely.

Meanwhile, in a medium saucepan, whisk together pineapple with juice and cornstarch until cornstarch has dissolved. Bring to a boil over high heat; boil for 1 to 2 minutes, or until thickened, whisking constantly. Remove from heat and allow to cool completely, 20 to 30 minutes.

To assemble, place one cooled cake layer on a serving plate, spread 1 cup whipped topping over cake, and spoon 1 cup cooled pineapple mixture over whipped topping. Place remaining cake layer on pineapple mixture; cover entire cake with remaining whipped topping, then spoon remaining pineapple mixture on top. Serve immediately or refrigerate for up to four days (cake tastes best if refrigerated for at least 4 hours to allow flavors to blend). To store, insert toothpicks on top and sides of cake and cover completely with plastic wrap (toothpicks will keep plastic wrap from sticking to cake); refrigerate.

VARIATION

This cake is best when layered, but you can turn it into a sheet cake if you prefer. Lightly spray a 13 x 9 x 2-inch cake pan with vegetable oil spray. Bake the cake at 350°F for about 40 minutes, or until a toothpick inserted in the center comes out clean, then let it cool. Spread the whipped topping evenly over the cake. Top with the pineapple mixture all the way to the edges. Refrigerate for at least 4 hours if time allows.

Calories 285
Protein 3 g
Carbohydrates 62 g
Fiber 1 g
Total Fat 2 g
  Saturated 1 g
  Polyunsaturated 0 g
  Monounsaturated 1 g
Cholesterol 0 mg
Sodium 336 mg

carrot cake with lemony cream cheese icing

Both baking powder and baking soda are used in this recipe. Why?
Baking powder aerates and lightens the batter, and baking soda helps neutralize
the acid in the buttermilk. The result is a delightful cake with a tangy, creamy topping.

Vegetable oil spray

cake

1½ cups all-purpose flour
1½ teaspoons baking powder
1½ teaspoons ground cinnamon
1   teaspoon baking soda
¾   cup firmly packed light brown sugar
2   tablespoons fat-free tub margarine, softened
¾   cup fat-free or low-fat buttermilk
    Whites of 3 large eggs

1   teaspoon vanilla extract
1½ cups grated carrots (4 to 5 medium)
½   cup raisins

icing

4   ounces reduced-fat cream cheese
4   ounces fat-free cream cheese
2   tablespoons fat-free tub margarine, chilled
1   teaspoon finely grated lemon zest
1   teaspoon vanilla extract
3   to 3½ cups sifted confectioners' sugar

Preheat oven to 350°F. Spray two 8-inch square or round cake pans with vegetable oil spray.

For cake, in a medium bowl, stir together flour, baking powder, cinnamon, and baking soda.

In a large mixing bowl, beat brown sugar and margarine with an electric mixer on medium until blended.

Add buttermilk, egg whites, and vanilla; beat on medium until well blended.

Gradually add flour mixture to buttermilk mixture, beating on low after each addition just until blended.

Fold in carrots and raisins. Divide batter evenly between two cake pans.

Bake for 20 to 25 minutes, or until a toothpick inserted in center comes out clean. Let stand on cooling racks for 10 minutes. Invert cakes onto racks, remove pans, and let cool completely.

Meanwhile, in a medium mixing bowl, combine icing ingredients except confectioners' sugar. Beat on low just until smooth (don't overbeat or icing will be too thin).

Calories 289
Protein 6 g
Carbohydrates 61 g
Fiber 1 g
Total Fat 3 g
 Saturated 2 g
 Polyunsaturated 0 g
 Monounsaturated 1 g
Cholesterol 9 mg
Sodium 327 mg

Gradually add 3 cups confectioners' sugar, beating on low until thick; add more confectioners' sugar if necessary to reach icinglike consistency. Transfer mixture to a shallow bowl, cover with plastic wrap, and refrigerate until thick and spreadable, about 1 hour.

To assemble, place one cake layer on a serving plate; spread ½ cup icing over top of cake only. Place second cake layer on first and spread remaining icing over top and sides. Cover loosely with plastic wrap and refrigerate until ready to serve.

COOK'S TIP: For additional fruit flavor, fold ¹⁄₂ cup finely chopped fresh or drained canned crushed pineapple (canned in its own juice) into the cake batter before baking.

COOK'S TIP ON STORING CAKES: Many times, as with this cake, you can make the cake, filling, and icing in advance, then wrap them separately in plastic wrap and refrigerate them for up to two days. Tightly wrapped in plastic wrap, the uniced cake can be frozen for up to one month; however, it is best not to freeze the icing. Let the cake thaw at room temperature before icing it.

triple-layer sponge cake with lemon cream filling

SERVES 12

Moist, sweet layers of sponge cake, tart lemon cream, and fluffy white icing make this cake light yet elegant.

cake

- 1¼ cups sifted cake flour
- 1¼ teaspoons baking powder
- ⅓ cup egg substitute, or 1 large egg plus white of 1 large egg
- 1 cup sugar
- ⅓ cup water
- 2 teaspoons vanilla extract
  Whites of 5 large eggs, room temperature
- ¼ cup sugar

filling

- ¼ cup plus 2 tablespoons sugar
- 3 tablespoons cornstarch
- 1⅓ cups fat-free milk
- 2 tablespoons light stick margarine
- 1 teaspoon finely grated lemon zest
- ¼ cup plus 1 to 2 tablespoons fresh lemon juice (about 2 medium lemons)

icing

- ¼ cup warm water
- 1 tablespoon plus 1 teaspoon powdered egg whites (pasteurized dried egg whites)
- 2 to 2½ cups sifted confectioners' sugar
- 1 teaspoon vanilla extract

Preheat oven to 350°F.

For cake, in a small bowl, thoroughly combine cake flour and baking powder. Set aside.

In a large mixing bowl, beat egg substitute with an electric mixer on high for 1 minute.

Gradually beat 1 cup sugar into egg substitute; beat on high for 4 minutes, or until mixture is thick and pale.

Add water and vanilla; beat on low until blended.

Gradually add flour mixture, beating on low after each addition until blended. Set aside.

In a large mixing bowl, beat egg whites on high until foamy.

Gradually beat in remaining ¼ cup sugar until stiff, glossy peaks form. (Peaks shouldn't fold over when beater is lifted, and meringue shouldn't feel grainy when rubbed with fingers.) Gently fold ½ cup egg white mixture into flour mixture. Fold in remaining egg white mixture until blended. Pour batter into an ungreased 10-inch tube pan.

Calories 258
Protein 5 g
Carbohydrates 58 g
Fiber 0 g
Total Fat 1 g
  Saturated 0 g
  Polyunsaturated 0 g
  Monounsaturated 0 g
Cholesterol 1 mg
Sodium 125 mg

Bake for 35 minutes, or until cake springs back when gently touched in center. Let cool completely on a cooling rack.

Meanwhile, for filling, combine sugar and cornstarch in a small saucepan.

Gradually whisk in milk until blended, then add margarine. Bring mixture to a boil over medium-high heat; boil until thick, about 1 minute, whisking constantly. Remove from heat.

Stir in lemon zest and lemon juice. Transfer filling to a medium glass bowl; place plastic wrap directly on filling and refrigerate until firm, 1 to 2 hours.

For icing, in a large mixing bowl, whisk together water and dried egg whites until egg whites are completely dissolved, about 2 minutes. Beat with an electric mixer on high until soft peaks form.

Gradually beat in 2 cups confectioners' sugar; beat until stiff peaks form, adding remaining confectioners' sugar if necessary to reach icinglike consistency.

Fold in vanilla.

To assemble, using a narrow metal spatula or knife, loosen cake from edge of pan, then remove cake from pan (if using a pan with removable bottom or if making cake ahead and refrigerating, leave cake attached to tube). Using a serrated knife, cut cake horizontally into three equal layers (remove layers from tube). Place bottom cake layer on serving plate and spread 1 cup lemon filling over layer. Top with second cake layer and remaining lemon filling. Place third cake layer on top and spread icing over top and sides. Serve immediately, or cover loosely with plastic wrap and refrigerate until ready to serve.

"hamburger" cake

SERVES 12 (WITH 1 YELLOW CAKE LAYER AND 1 GERMAN CHOCOLATE CAKE LAYER REMAINING)

Hamburger for dessert? You bet, when the "bun" is yellow cake, the "hamburger" is German chocolate cake, and the toppings are colored whipped topping for mustard, confectioners' sugar glaze for mayonnaise, kiwifruit for pickles, and strawberries for tomatoes. This is the perfect cake for a child's birthday party.

yellow cake layer

- 1 18.25-ounce box reduced-fat yellow cake mix
- 1 1/3 cups water
   Egg substitute equivalent to 3 eggs
- 2 tablespoons unsweetened applesauce

german chocolate cake layer

- 1 18.25-ounce box German chocolate cake mix
- 1 1/4 cups water
   Egg substitute equivalent to 3 eggs
- 1/3 cup unsweetened applesauce

❖

- 1 cup confectioners' sugar, sifted
- 1 to 3 tablespoons fat-free milk
- 1 cup frozen fat-free or light whipped topping, thawed (about 3 ounces)
- 6 to 8 drops yellow food coloring
- 1 cup hulled and sliced strawberries (about 1/2 pint)
- 4 medium kiwifruit, peeled and thinly sliced (about 24 slices)
- 1 tablespoon poppy or sesame seeds (optional)

Prepare yellow cake using package directions for two 8-inch round cakes, or for 1 round cake and 12 cupcakes for use in Boston Cream Cupcakes, page 28, substituting egg substitute for whole eggs and applesauce for oil. (You'll need only one round yellow cake layer for this recipe.)

Prepare German chocolate cake using package directions for two 8-inch round cakes, or for 1 round cake and 12 cupcakes for another use, substituting egg substitute for whole eggs and applesauce for oil. (You'll need only one round German chocolate cake layer for this recipe.)

Using a sharp knife, cut one yellow cake layer in half horizontally. With a large spatula or cake mover, remove and set aside top half of cake. Place bottom half on serving plate.

Put confectioners' sugar in a small bowl. Gradually pour in milk, whisking after each addition, until mixture will drizzle from a spoon (mixture should not be too thin). Drizzle on bottom half of cake.

Top with one German chocolate cake layer.

Put whipped topping in a small bowl; stir in food coloring until it reaches desired color for "mustard." Spread over German chocolate cake layer.

Calories 243
Protein 4 g
Carbohydrates 52 g
Fiber 2 g
Total Fat 3 g
  Saturated 1 g
  Polyunsaturated 0 g
  Monounsaturated 1 g
Cholesterol 0 mg
Sodium 310 mg

Arrange strawberries and kiwifruit over whipped topping.

Carefully place remaining half yellow cake layer on fruit; sprinkle with poppy or sesame seeds. Components of cake can be prepared up to two days in advance (refrigerate glaze, whipped topping, and fruit), then assembled and refrigerated up to 8 hours before serving.

COOK'S TIP: The applesauce and egg substitute called for in this recipe are replacements for the oil and whole eggs specified on the cake mix package. If your cake mix lists different amounts for oil, whole eggs, or water, use those amounts.

COOK'S TIP ON CAKE MOVER: A cake mover is a handy gadget that looks like a large, wide spatula. Slide it between cut layers of cake to move them easily without breaking the cake into pieces. Look for it in gourmet shops or stores that sell cake decorating supplies.

banana cake with chocolate pudding topping

SERVES 16

This moist cake tastes like a chocolate-covered banana. For a totally different taste, substitute vanilla pudding mix for the chocolate fudge.

Butter-flavor vegetable oil spray

cake

- 3 very ripe medium bananas
- 1/2 cup nonfat or light sour cream
- 1 1/4 cups sugar
- 1/4 cup plus 2 tablespoons light tub margarine
- Whites of 2 large eggs
- 1 large egg (not egg substitute)
- 2 cups all-purpose flour
- 1 teaspoon baking powder
- 1 teaspoon baking soda

pudding

- 1 small package sugar-free, fat-free (about 1 ounce) or regular (about 3.4 ounces) instant chocolate fudge pudding
- 2 cups fat-free milk

Preheat oven to 350°F. Spray an 11 × 7 × 1½-inch, 12 × 8 × 2-inch, or other 8- to 10-cup baking pan with vegetable oil spray.

In a food processor or blender, process bananas until almost smooth.

Add sour cream and process until smooth. Set aside.

In a large mixing bowl, with an electric mixer on medium, cream sugar and margarine together until fluffy, about 2 minutes.

Beat in egg whites and egg.

In a medium bowl, sift together remaining cake ingredients. Add alternately with banana mixture to sugar mixture, beating after each addition. Pour into baking pan.

Bake for 35 to 40 minutes, or until cake is golden brown and a toothpick inserted in center comes out clean, rotating cake once about halfway through baking time. Let cool almost completely on cooling rack, 30 to 40 minutes.

Meanwhile, prepare pudding according to package directions but using 2 cups fat-free milk.

Just before serving, spread pudding over top of cake, swirling to make an attractive design. Cake can be made one day ahead, but don't top with pudding until ready to serve.

Calories 185
Protein 4 g
Carbohydrates 37 g
Fiber 1 g
Total Fat 2 g
  Saturated 0 g
  Polyunsaturated 1 g
  Monounsaturated 1 g
Cholesterol 15 mg
Sodium 250 mg

banana bonanza cake

Dress up store-bought angel food cake with layers of creamy, fluffy pudding mixture, fresh banana slices, and a hint of nutmeg for a quick rich-tasting dessert.

1   9-inch angel food cake
1½ cups fat-free milk
1   small package sugar-free, fat-free (about 1 ounce) or regular (about 3.4 ounces) instant vanilla pudding mix
4   ounces reduced-fat cream cheese (not fat free)

8   ounces frozen fat-free or light whipped topping, thawed (about 3 cups)
4   medium bananas, unpeeled (about 1½ pounds), divided use
½   teaspoon ground nutmeg, divided use

With a long serrated knife, cut cake horizontally into three equal layers. Set aside.

Pour milk into a medium mixing bowl; add pudding mix. Using an electric mixer, beat on low for 2 minutes, or until thickened.

Add cream cheese. Beat on high setting until smooth.

Using a rubber scraper, gently fold in whipped topping until well blended.

To assemble, put bottom layer of cake on a large plate. Spread with 1 cup pudding mixture. Peel and slice one banana over pudding, then sprinkle banana slices with about ⅛ teaspoon nutmeg. Repeat, being careful to center second layer over first layer. Top with remaining layer of cake; cover entire cake with remaining pudding mixture. Insert toothpicks on top and sides of cake and cover completely with plastic wrap (toothpicks will keep plastic wrap from sticking to pudding). Refrigerate for 8 hours or overnight.

To serve, slice remaining two bananas and decoratively arrange on top and sides of cake; lightly sprinkle with remaining ¼ teaspoon nutmeg.

COOK'S TIP: You can add the bananas for the top and sides of the cake up to 3 hours before serving, then wrap the cake with plastic wrap and refrigerate it. If you add the bananas sooner, they may discolor. Be sure to keep the cake wrapped until serving time to prevent discoloration.

Calories 218
Protein 5 g
Carbohydrates 43 g
Fiber 1 g
Total Fat 3 g
  Saturated 2 g
  Polyunsaturated 0 g
  Monounsaturated 1 g
Cholesterol 8 mg
Sodium 234 mg

almond torte
with chocolate ganache

Because the almonds that replace part of the flour in this cake are heavier than flour, this torte does not rise much. It's still rich, moist, and dense, though. The ganache uses fat-free nondairy creamer instead of heavy cream—and the result is a super-rich filling that tastes positively decadent.

Vegetable oil spray

torte

- ¼ cup sliced almonds
- 1 cup all-purpose flour
- 1 teaspoon baking powder
- 1 cup sugar
  Egg substitute equivalent to 4 eggs
- 2 tablespoons fat-free tub margarine, melted
- 1 teaspoon vanilla extract
- 1 teaspoon almond extract

ganache

- ⅔ cup reduced-fat semisweet chocolate chips (about 4 ounces)
- ½ cup fat-free French vanilla liquid nondairy creamer
- 3 tablespoons whipped topping mix (from 1.3-ounce envelope)
- ¼ cup fat-free milk, chilled (see Cook's Tip, page 17)

topping

- 1 tablespoon confectioners' sugar
- ½ teaspoon unsweetened cocoa powder (Dutch process preferred)

Preheat oven to 325°F. Spray two 9-inch round cake pans with vegetable oil spray. Set aside.

For torte, in a food processor, process almonds until finely chopped.

Add flour and baking powder; process until blended.

In a large mixing bowl, combine sugar and egg substitute. Beat with an electric mixer on high for 4 minutes, or until mixture is thick and pale.

Beat in margarine and vanilla and almond extracts.

With mixer on low, gradually beat in flour mixture until blended. Divide batter evenly between two pans.

Bake for 20 to 25 minutes, or until a toothpick inserted in center comes out clean or top is golden and cakes begin to pull away from sides of pans. Let stand on cooling racks for 10 minutes. Invert cakes onto racks, remove pans, and let cakes cool completely.

Meanwhile, for ganache, melt chocolate chips in top of a double boiler or medium glass bowl over simmering water (water shouldn't touch bottom of pan). Set aside to cool slightly.

Calories 196
Protein 4 g
Carbohydrates 38 g
Fiber 1 g
Total Fat 3 g
  Saturated 2 g
  Polyunsaturated 0 g
  Monounsaturated 1 g
Cholesterol 0 mg
Sodium 94 mg

low-fat & luscious desserts

In a small saucepan, heat creamer over medium heat just until bubbles appear around edge. Whisk into melted chocolate until smooth. Cover and refrigerate until cool, about 1 hour.

In a large mixing bowl, combine whipped topping mix and milk. Beat with an electric mixer on low until blended. Increase setting to high and beat until stiff peaks form, about 4 minutes. Fold gently into cooled chocolate mixture and refrigerate until ready to use.

To assemble torte, put one cake layer on serving platter and spread ganache on top only. Place second cake layer on ganache. In a small bowl, combine topping ingredients. Transfer mixture to a fine sieve and sprinkle over torte. Using a serrated knife, gently slice torte into wedges. (A heavy hand will force the ganache from between the cake layers.)

COOK'S TIP: If you don't have a food processor, grind the almonds in a coffee grinder or put them in an airtight plastic bag and mash them with a meat mallet.

COOK'S TIP ON LIQUID NONDAIRY CREAMER: The various flavors of liquid nondairy creamer, found near the milk in the refrigerated section of the grocery, are a fat-free way to perk up your coffee. A more unusual use is as a flavorful ingredient in baked goods, as in this recipe.

pumpkin spice cake
with white chocolate icing

A combination of white chocolate and sour cream makes a slightly tart icing that is a terrific partner for this pumpkin-flavored spice cake. For a different but equally delicious taste, try Fudge Icing (page 100) instead.

Vegetable oil spray

cake

2	cups all-purpose flour
¾	cup sugar
2½	teaspoons baking powder
2	teaspoons ground cinnamon
1	teaspoon baking soda
¾	teaspoon ground cloves
¼	teaspoon ground ginger
1	15-ounce can solid-pack pumpkin (not pie filling)
	Egg substitute equivalent to 2 eggs, or 2 large eggs

⅓	cup unsweetened applesauce
⅓	cup fat-free milk
2	tablespoons fat-free tub margarine, melted

icing

2	tablespoons fat-free tub margarine
½	cup sugar
¼	cup white chocolate chips
3	tablespoons fat-free milk
2	cups sifted confectioners' sugar
1	teaspoon vanilla extract

Preheat oven to 350°F. Spray a 9-inch round cake pan with vegetable oil spray. Set aside.

For cake, in a large bowl, use a whisk or fork to thoroughly combine flour, sugar, baking powder, cinnamon, baking soda, cloves, and ginger. Make a well in center.

In a medium bowl, whisk together remaining cake ingredients. Pour into center of dry ingredients; whisk together until well blended. Pour batter into cake pan and smooth top.

Bake for 40 minutes, or until a toothpick inserted in center comes out clean. Let stand on a cooling rack for 10 minutes. Remove cake from pan and let cool completely, right side up, on cooling rack.

Meanwhile, for icing, melt margarine in a small saucepan over medium-low heat.

Calories 269
Protein 4 g
Carbohydrates 60 g
Fiber 2 g
Total Fat 1 g
  Saturated 1 g
  Polyunsaturated 0 g
  Monounsaturated 0 g
Cholesterol 1 mg
Sodium 265 mg

Whisk in sugar, white chocolate chips, and milk. Cook for 2 minutes, or until smooth, whisking constantly. Transfer to a medium glass bowl and place plastic wrap directly on surface. Refrigerate for 30 minutes, or until cool.

Whisk in remaining ingredients until blended. Spread icing over top and sides of cooled cake.

pecan shortcake with peach melba sauce

SERVES 8; 1 WEDGE SHORTCAKE AND SCANT $^1/_2$ CUP SAUCE PER SERVING

*Serve this easy-to-prepare shortcake at a summer picnic or barbecue.
The colorful sauce is terrific over fat-free ice cream or sherbet as well.*

Vegetable oil spray (optional)

shortcake

- 2 cups all-purpose flour
- $^1/_3$ cup sugar
- 2 teaspoons baking powder
- 1 teaspoon ground cinnamon
- $^1/_4$ teaspoon ground nutmeg
- 3 tablespoons plus 1$^1/_2$ teaspoons light stick margarine
- 2 tablespoons unsweetened applesauce
- $^1/_4$ cup nuts, such as pecans, chopped and dry-roasted (see Cook's Tip on Dry-Roasting Nuts, page 68)

- $^1/_3$ cup fat-free milk
- Egg substitute equivalent to 1 egg, or 1 large egg
- 1 to 2 tablespoons all-purpose flour for kneading

peach melba sauce

- 5 medium peaches (about 1$^1/_4$ pounds), peeled and sliced into wedges
- $^3/_4$ pint fresh raspberries (about 1$^1/_4$ cups)
- $^3/_4$ cup sugar
- $^3/_4$ cup water
- 1 tablespoon plus 1$^1/_2$ teaspoons cornstarch
- 3 tablespoons cold water

Preheat oven to 425°F. Line a baking sheet with cooking parchment, or spray baking sheet with vegetable oil spray. Set aside.

For shortcake, in a large bowl, combine 2 cups flour, sugar, baking powder, cinnamon, and nutmeg.

Add margarine in small chunks. Using a pastry blender, two knives, or a fork, blend until margarine is in pea-size pieces.

Stir in remaining shortcake ingredients except flour for kneading. Press dough together. Sprinkle with remaining flour if dough is sticky. Knead it for a few turns. Place dough on baking sheet and press into an 8-inch circle about $^1/_4$ inch thick. Cut dough into eight wedges.

Bake for 12 to 15 minutes, or until tops are lightly browned.

Meanwhile, for sauce, in a medium, heavy saucepan, bring peaches, raspberries, sugar, and $^3/_4$ cup water to a boil over medium heat.

Put cornstarch in a small bowl. Add cold water, stirring to dissolve. Pour into peach mixture and cook until mixture begins to thicken and becomes clear, 2 to 3 minutes, whisking constantly. Let cool slightly.

To serve, pour about $^1/_4$ cup sauce onto each of eight dessert plates. Place cake on each plate, then pour about $^1/_4$ cup sauce over each piece.

Calories 325
Protein 6 g
Carbohydrates 65 g
Fiber 4 g
Total Fat 5 g
  Saturated 1 g
  Polyunsaturated 2 g
  Monounsaturated 2 g
Cholesterol 0 mg
Sodium 188 mg

apple cappuccino cake

Dust this moist, flavorful cake with confectioners' sugar, or crown it with Mocha Frosting (page 157). It would be delightful at your next coffee klatch or brunch.

Vegetable oil spray

2 cups chopped tart apples, such as Pippin, Jonathan, or Granny Smith (about 2 large or 3 medium)

²/₃ cup sugar

1 cup all-purpose flour

1 tablespoon unsweetened cocoa powder (Dutch process preferred) (optional)

1 teaspoon ground cinnamon

½ teaspoon baking powder

½ teaspoon baking soda

¼ teaspoon salt

¼ cup coffee

Egg substitute equivalent to 1 egg, or 1 large egg

2 tablespoons acceptable vegetable oil

1 teaspoon instant coffee granules

1 teaspoon vanilla extract

Confectioners' sugar for dusting cake (optional)

Preheat oven to 350°F. Spray an 8- or 9-inch square baking pan with vegetable oil spray. Set aside.

In a medium bowl, stir together apples and sugar; let stand for 10 minutes.

Meanwhile, in a large bowl, stir together flour, optional cocoa powder, cinnamon, baking powder, baking soda, and salt.

In a medium bowl, stir together remaining ingredients except confectioners' sugar.

Stir apple mixture into flour mixture.

Add coffee mixture, stirring just until blended. Pour batter into pan.

Bake for 20 to 25 minutes, or until a toothpick inserted in center comes out clean.

Let cool on a rack for about 30 minutes. To serve, remove pan and dust cake with confectioners' sugar and cut into squares.

COOK'S TIP: If using the Mocha Frosting, spread it over the cake while the cake is warm.

WITHOUT FROSTING
Calories 158
Protein 2 g
Carbohydrates 30 g
Fiber 1 g
Total Fat 3 g
Saturated 0 g
Polyunsaturated 2 g
Monounsaturated 1 g
Cholesterol 0 mg
Sodium 174 mg

apple cinnamon cake

Moist and easy to make, this cake is great for breakfast or tea.

Vegetable oil spray
2 ¼ cups all-purpose flour
1 teaspoon baking soda
1 teaspoon ground cinnamon
½ teaspoon ground cloves
½ teaspoon ground allspice
½ teaspoon ground nutmeg
¼ teaspoon salt
½ cup firmly packed light brown sugar
½ cup light stick margarine, melted

½ cup light corn syrup
½ cup unsweetened applesauce
Whites of 4 large eggs, lightly beaten
1 teaspoon vanilla extract
⅓ cup fat-free or low-fat buttermilk
2 cups peeled and chopped tart apples, such as Pippin or Granny Smith, or pears (about 3 medium)
1 cup chopped dates (about 8 ounces pitted)
Confectioners' sugar for dusting

Preheat oven to 350°F. Spray a Bundt pan with vegetable oil spray. Set aside.

In a large bowl, sift together flour, baking soda, cinnamon, cloves, allspice, nutmeg, and salt.

In another large bowl, stir together brown sugar, margarine, corn syrup, applesauce, egg whites, and vanilla. Gradually add flour mixture, alternating with buttermilk, stirring well after each addition.

Stir in apples and dates. Pour batter into pan.

Bake for 1 hour to 1 hour 10 minutes, or until a toothpick inserted in center comes out clean. Let stand on a cooling rack for 10 minutes. Invert cake onto a platter, remove pan, and dust cake with confectioners' sugar. Serve warm or at room temperature.

Calories 194
Protein 3 g
Carbohydrates 40 g
Fiber 2 g
Total Fat 3 g
  Saturated 1 g
  Polyunsaturated 1 g
  Monounsaturated 1 g
Cholesterol 0 mg
Sodium 188 mg

low-fat & luscious desserts

apple snack cake

This is definitely an apple-lover's fantasy fulfilled—a spice cake jam-packed with fresh apple slices and topped with cinnamon sugar.

Vegetable oil spray
6 medium Granny Smith apples (about 2 pounds)
1 8.25-ounce box spice cake mix or carrot cake mix
1 cup water
1 6-ounce jar pureed sweet potato or carrot baby food

2 large eggs (not egg substitute)
Whites of 2 large eggs
1/2 teaspoon ground nutmeg
1 teaspoon vanilla, butter, and nut flavoring or vanilla extract
2 tablespoons sugar
1/4 teaspoon ground cinnamon

Preheat oven to 325°F. Lightly spray a 13 × 9 × 2-inch nonstick baking pan with vegetable oil spray. Set aside.

Peel, core, and thinly slice apples; set aside in a medium mixing bowl.

In a large mixing bowl, combine cake mix, water, sweet potatoes, eggs, egg whites, nutmeg, and flavoring. Using an electric mixer, beat on low to moisten ingredients, about 30 seconds. Increase to medium and beat for 2 minutes.

Using a rubber scraper, fold apples into batter, blending well. Pour batter into pan.

Bake for 1 hour, or until a toothpick inserted in center comes out clean. Let cool completely on a cooling rack.

Meanwhile, in a small bowl, stir together sugar and cinnamon.

To serve, cut cake into pieces and sprinkle each with 1/4 teaspoon of cinnamon sugar. Refrigerate remaining cake in an airtight nonmetal container. Cake is best if eaten within 24 hours.

COOK'S TIP: Because of the moistness of the cake, the cinnamon sugar will dissolve after about 4 hours. For peak flavors, wait until serving time to add it.

Calories 128
Protein 2 g
Carbohydrates 23 g
Fiber 1 g
Total Fat 3 g
  Saturated 1 g
  Polyunsaturated 0 g
  Monounsaturated 1 g
Cholesterol 32 mg
Sodium 174 mg

farmer's market snack cake

Sneak nutrition into your kids' snacks with this moist cake. It cleverly disguises nutrient-packed vegetables as a dessert treat. This not-too-sweet cake is thick and dense, so a small square is very filling.

Vegetable oil spray
1½ cups all-purpose flour
½ to ¾ cup sugar
1 teaspoon baking soda
½ cup shredded zucchini
½ cup shredded carrot
½ cup shredded sweet potato
3 tablespoons chopped walnuts

½ cup pineapple juice
Egg substitute equivalent to 1 egg, or 1 large egg
1 tablespoon acceptable vegetable oil
1 teaspoon ground cinnamon
1 teaspoon vanilla extract
1 cup peach butter or apple butter

Preheat oven to 325°F. Spray an 8-inch square baking pan with vegetable oil spray.

In a large bowl, stir together flour, sugar, and baking soda.

Stir in zucchini, carrot, sweet potato, and walnuts.

Add remaining ingredients except peach butter; stir just until combined (batter will be slightly lumpy). Pour into baking pan.

Bake for 30 minutes, or until a toothpick inserted in center comes out clean. Let cool for about 10 minutes, then cut into 2-inch squares. Place each square on a dessert plate; spread each square with 1 tablespoon peach butter.

COOK'S TIP: The next time you're at a farmer's market, stock up on different fruits and vegetables that will work well in this cake. You'll need 1½ cups peeled, grated raw parsnips, butternut or acorn squash, apples, pears, or pumpkin, or unpeeled crookneck squash.

COOK'S TIP ON FRUIT BUTTER: Fruit butter can be found near the jellies in your grocery. Even though this thick, spreadable mixture calls itself "butter," it isn't. It's cooked fruit with sugar, spices, and a small amount of vinegar.

Calories 135
Protein 2 g
Carbohydrates 28 g
Fiber 1 g
Total Fat 2 g
  Saturated 0 g
  Polyunsaturated 1 g
  Monounsaturated 0 g
Cholesterol 0 mg
Sodium 90 mg

maui cheesecake

You'll feel as if you're on a paradise island when you savor this pineapple cheesecake with its hint of papaya and macadamia nuts.

crust

- 1 cup crushed reduced-fat vanilla wafers (about 36)
- 1/3 cup crushed macadamia nuts (about 1 1/3 ounces)
- 1 tablespoon all-purpose flour
- 1/4 cup sugar

filling

- 16 ounces fat-free or low-fat cottage cheese
- 16 ounces fat-free or low-fat vanilla yogurt
- 8 ounces fat-free cream cheese
- 4 ounces reduced-fat cream cheese
- 1 cup sugar
- Egg substitute equivalent to 2 eggs, or 2 large eggs
- 1/4 cup all-purpose flour
- 1 8-ounce can crushed pineapple in its own juice, drained
- 1/2 medium papaya or mango, diced, or 1/2 cup diced canned papaya or mango rinsed and drained
- 2 teaspoons vanilla extract

❖

- 1/2 medium papaya or mango, sliced (optional)
- Fresh pineapple slices or sliced pineapple canned in its own juice, drained (optional)
- Frozen fat-free or light whipped topping, thawed (optional)

Preheat oven to 350°F. Spray a 9-inch springform pan.

For crust, combine all ingredients in a medium bowl. Pat onto bottom of pan.

For filling, put cottage cheese in a colander and rinse. Drain well, gently pressing cheese with back of a spoon to squeeze out as much liquid as possible. Pat dry with paper towels. In a food processor, process cottage cheese until smooth, stopping occasionally to scrape sides.

Add yogurt, cream cheeses, sugar, egg substitute, and flour; process until smooth.

Fold in remaining ingredients. Pour into pan.

Bake for 1 hour 15 minutes to 1 hour 30 minutes, or until firm around edges and set in center (doesn't jiggle when cheesecake is gently shaken). Turn off oven and let cheesecake stand in oven with door closed for 30 minutes. Remove from oven and let cool completely on a cooling rack, about 2 1/2 hours. Remove springform pan sides. Cover cheesecake with plastic wrap and refrigerate for at least 4 hours.

To serve, decorate cheesecake with remaining papaya, sliced pineapple, and dollops of whipped topping.

Calories 282
Protein 12 g
Carbohydrates 46 g
Fiber 1 g
Total Fat 5 g
  Saturated 2 g
  Polyunsaturated 0 g
  Monounsaturated 3 g
Cholesterol 13 mg
Sodium 310 mg

cheesecake with fresh berry sauce

SERVES 12

Lindy's restaurant in New York City is credited with making cheesecake famous. You'll be pleasantly surprised at our version's richness, even though it weighs in at just 4 grams of fat per serving (compared to 48 grams in a slice of the original).

Vegetable oil spray

crust

1 cup finely crushed low-fat graham cracker crumbs (cinnamon preferred) (about 16 squares)
2 tablespoons coarsely chopped pecans
1 tablespoon light stick margarine, melted

filling

16 ounces fat-free or low-fat cottage cheese (2 cups)
16 ounces fat-free or low-fat vanilla yogurt (2 cups)
8 ounces fat-free cream cheese
4 ounces reduced-fat cream cheese

1 cup sugar
Egg substitute equivalent to 2 eggs, or 2 large eggs
¼ cup all-purpose flour
1 teaspoon vanilla extract
1 teaspoon finely shredded lemon zest

sauce

1 quart fresh strawberries or fresh raspberries (about 4 cups)
½ cup sugar

❖

Fresh strawberries, raspberries, or blueberries (optional)

Preheat oven to 300°F. Spray a 9-inch springform pan with vegetable oil spray.

For crust, in a food processor, process crumbs, pecans, and margarine until well blended or combine with a spoon. Press crumb mixture onto bottom of springform pan. Bake for 5 minutes. Let crust cool on a cooling rack, leaving oven on.

Meanwhile, for filling, put cottage cheese in a colander and rinse. Drain well, gently pressing cheese with back of a spoon to squeeze out as much liquid as possible. Pat dry with paper towels. In a food processor or blender, process cottage cheese until smooth, stopping occasionally to scrape sides.

Calories 273
Protein 12 g
Carbohydrates 47 g
Fiber 2 g
Total Fat 4 g
  Saturated 2 g
  Polyunsaturated 1 g
  Monounsaturated 1 g
Cholesterol 13 mg
Sodium 314 mg

Add remaining filling ingredients; process until smooth. Carefully pour over cooled crust.

Bake for 1 hour to 1 hour 15 minutes, or until firm around edges but still slightly wobbly in center. Turn off oven and let cheesecake stand in oven with door closed for 30 minutes. Remove from oven and let cool completely on a cooling rack, 1½ to 2 hours. Remove springform pan sides. Cover cheesecake with plastic wrap and refrigerate for at least 4 hours.

In a food processor or blender, process sauce ingredients until smooth. Strain through a sieve to remove seeds if desired.

Spoon half the sauce onto 12 dessert plates. Slice cheesecake into 12 pieces. Place each slice on a plate. Drizzle each serving with remaining sauce. If you prefer, divide entire recipe of sauce among plates and place cheesecake on top. Garnish with fresh berries.

boston cream cupcakes

SERVES 12 (WITH 1 CAKE LAYER OR 12 PLAIN CUPCAKES REMAINING)

*A classic cake goes miniature. You'll have extra batter for "Hamburger" Cake (page 12),
or you can make additional cupcakes to top with one of our icings or dessert sauces.*

cupcakes/cake

- 1   18.25-ounce box reduced-fat yellow cake mix
- 1¼   cups water
-      Egg substitute equivalent to 3 eggs
- ⅓   cup unsweetened applesauce

custard

- 1   vanilla bean
- 1   cup fat-free milk
- ½   cup sugar
-      Egg substitute equivalent to 1 egg
- 3   tablespoons cornstarch
- 1   tablespoon rum or 1 teaspoon rum extract

chocolate glaze

- 1   cup confectioners' sugar, sifted
- 2   tablespoons unsweetened cocoa powder (Dutch process preferred), sifted
- 2   to 3 tablespoons strong coffee

Prepare cake using package directions for cupcakes, substituting egg substitute for whole eggs and applesauce for oil. Pour 3 cups batter into muffin cups for this recipe. (To use the extra batter for "Hamburger" Cake [see page 12], also spray a nonstick 8-inch round cake pan with vegetable oil spray. For extra cupcakes, spray a second muffin pan.)

Bake according to package directions, or until a toothpick inserted in center of cupcake comes out clean. Remove from pan and let cool completely on a cooling rack.

For custard, split vanilla bean in half and scrape out seeds with a knife. Put seeds and scraped pod in top of a double boiler.

Whisk in remaining custard ingredients except rum. Cook over simmering water for 3 to 4 minutes, or until mixture starts to thicken, whisking occasionally (water shouldn't touch bottom of pan). Continue cooking until custard is thick and smooth, about 1 minute, whisking constantly. Discard vanilla bean pod.

Add rum and cook for 1 minute, whisking occasionally. Remove top of double boiler from heat and let custard cool for 10 to 15 minutes. (Use custard as soon as it is lukewarm or transfer to a medium bowl, place plastic wrap directly on custard, and refrigerate for up to four days.)

Calories 174
Protein 3 g
Carbohydrates 39 g
Fiber 0 g
Total Fat 1 g
  Saturated 0 g
  Polyunsaturated 0 g
  Monounsaturated 0 g
Cholesterol 0 mg
Sodium 173 mg

For glaze, stir together confectioners' sugar and cocoa powder in a small bowl. Gradually pour in coffee, whisking after each addition, until mixture is spreadable but not too thin.

To assemble, cut a cupcake in half horizontally. Place bottom half on a plate. Spread 1 heaping tablespoon custard on cupcake. Frost top half of cupcake with glaze; place on custard. Repeat with remaining ingredients. Refrigerate any leftover cupcakes in an airtight container for up to two days.

COOK'S TIP: The applesauce and egg substitute called for in this recipe are replacements for the oil and whole eggs specified on the cake mix package. If your cake mix lists different amounts for oil, whole eggs, or water, use those amounts.

Pecan-Pie Cookies

Jewel Thumbprint Cookies

No-Bake Oatmeal Raisin Cookies

No-Bake Oatmeal Raisin Bars

Almond and Blueberry Cookies

Oatmeal Lace Cookies

Brandy Orange Snaps

Drop Sugar Cookies

Frosted Pineapple Cookies

Butterscotchers

Pumpkin Nutmeg Cookies

Ginger Nut Cookies

Cherry Oat Cookies

Gingerbread Window Cookies

Trail Mix Squares

Lemon-Date Bars

Lemony Lime Squares

Raspberry Blondies

Raspberry Brownies

the
cookie
jar

pecan-pie cookies

SERVES 25; 2 COOKIES PER SERVING

The surprise topping on these cookies is just like pecan pie.

cookies

- 4 cups all-purpose flour
- 1 teaspoon baking soda
- 1/4 teaspoon salt
- 2 cups firmly packed light or dark brown sugar
- 1 cup light tub margarine, softened
- 1 large egg (not egg substitute)
  White of 1 large egg
- 2 teaspoons vanilla extract

topping

- 3/4 cup chopped pecans
- 1/2 cup plus 2 tablespoons firmly packed dark brown sugar
- 1/4 cup plus 2 tablespoons nonfat or light sour cream
  Vegetable oil spray (optional)

For cookies, in a large bowl, sift together flour, baking soda, and salt. Set aside.

In a large mixing bowl, beat brown sugar and margarine with an electric mixer on medium for about 2 minutes, or until creamy.

Add remaining cookie ingredients, beating until incorporated.

Gradually add flour mixture to brown sugar mixture, beating after each addition just until well blended. Refrigerate for 20 to 30 minutes to firm up.

Meanwhile, in a small bowl, stir together topping ingredients. Set aside.

Preheat oven to 350°F. Line two baking sheets with cooking parchment, or spray baking sheets with vegetable oil spray.

Roll dough into 1-inch balls. Place 2 inches apart on baking sheets and press flat with palm of hand to about 1½ inches in diameter. Using your thumb, make a depression in center of each cookie. Spoon about 1½ teaspoons topping into each depression.

Bake for 12 to 14 minutes, or until cookies start to lightly brown. Transfer cookies, still on cooking parchment, to cooling rack; let cool for about 15 minutes.

COOK'S TIP ON COOKIE SHEETS: If you use a thin baking sheet, it's important to switch it front to back about halfway through the baking time. If you're using two sheets, also switch them top to bottom.

Calories 221
Protein 3 g
Carbohydrates 41 g
Fiber 1 g
Total Fat 5 g
  Saturated 1 g
  Polyunsaturated 2 g
  Monounsaturated 2 g
Cholesterol 9 mg
Sodium 136 mg

jewel thumbprint cookies

Children love helping with these cookies and give them a thumbs-up!

2 1/2 cups all-purpose flour
1/2 teaspoon baking powder
1/2 teaspoon salt
3/4 cup sugar
  Egg substitute equivalent to 2 eggs, or 2 large eggs
1/3 cup unsweetened applesauce
1/4 cup acceptable vegetable oil
1 1/2 teaspoons vanilla extract
  Flour for rolling dough
3 tablespoons all-fruit preserves, such as apricot or blackberry
2 tablespoons confectioners' sugar

Preheat oven to 350°F.

In a medium bowl, stir together flour, baking powder, and salt.

In a large mixing bowl, with an electric mixer on medium-high, beat sugar, egg substitute, applesauce, oil, and vanilla until light and fluffy.

Gradually stir flour mixture into sugar mixture, forming a soft dough. Lightly flour your hands and roll heaping teaspoonfuls of dough into 36 small balls. Place 2 inches apart on ungreased baking sheets. Dip bottom of a glass in flour and flatten cookies to 1/2-inch thickness.

Make thumbprint in center of each cookie. Fill each center with 1/4 teaspoon preserves.

Bake for 10 minutes, or until cookies are firm and preserves are bubbly. Transfer cookies from baking sheets to cooling racks. When cookies are cool, sift confectioners' sugar over them. Store in an air-tight container, separating layers of cookies with sheets of wax paper, for up to one week.

Calories 136
Protein 3 g
Carbohydrates 24 g
Fiber 1 g
Total Fat 3 g
  Saturated 0 g
  Polyunsaturated 2 g
  Monounsaturated 1 g
Cholesterol 0 mg
Sodium 93 mg

no-bake oatmeal raisin cookies

SERVES 12; 2 COOKIES PER SERVING

Not just for dessert, these easy-to-make, chewy gems are also good for between-meal hunger pangs. For variety, add dry-roasted almond slivers or reduced-fat chocolate chips. (Just remember that the calorie count and the nutrient amounts will increase.)

2 1/2 cups quick-cooking oatmeal, uncooked
1 cup raisins or minced dried fruit
3/4 cup honey
1/4 cup reduced-fat creamy or chunky peanut butter

1/4 cup unsweetened applesauce
1 teaspoon ground cinnamon
1 teaspoon vanilla extract or almond extract
1/3 cup whole-wheat flour

In a large bowl, stir together all ingredients except flour until well blended. Roll dough into 24 balls.

Put flour on a small plate. Roll cookies in flour, making sure to coat completely; shake off excess flour. Place cookies on ungreased baking sheets. Lightly flour your hands and press cookies gently with your fingers to flatten slightly, to about 2 inches in diameter. Refrigerate cookies until firm, about 30 minutes. Refrigerate leftover cookies in an airtight plastic container for up to three days.

NO-BAKE OATMEAL RAISIN BARS

Dust the bottom of an $11 \times 7 \times 1\frac{1}{2}$-inch baking dish with whole-wheat flour. Using a piece of plastic wrap to prevent mixture from sticking to your hands, press prepared cookie dough onto the bottom of the baking dish. Lightly dust bars with whole-wheat flour. Refrigerate until firm, about 1 hour. Cut into 24 squares. Serves 12; 2 cookies per serving.

COOK'S TIP: For a richer flavor, try toasting the uncooked oatmeal before adding it to the other ingredients. Preheat the oven to 350°F. Spread the oatmeal on an ungreased rimmed baking sheet. Bake for 10 to 15 minutes, or until golden, shaking pan halfway through cooking for even browning.

Calories 209
Protein 5 g
Carbohydrates 44 g
Fiber 3 g
Total Fat 3 g
  Saturated 1 g
  Polyunsaturated 1 g
  Monounsaturated 1 g
Cholesterol 0 mg
Sodium 33 mg

almond and blueberry cookies

One bite and you'll be hooked on the unusual flavor of these cookies.

Vegetable oil spray (optional)
1 1/4 cups blanched almonds
1 1/2 cups sugar
1 1/8 cups all-purpose flour
3/4 cup dried blueberries or other minced
    dried fruit

Whites of 3 large eggs
3/4 teaspoon almond extract
1/2 teaspoon vanilla extract

Preheat oven to 350°F. Spray two heavy nonstick baking sheets with vegetable oil spray or line with cooking parchment.

In a food processor or blender, process almonds until coarsely ground; transfer to a large bowl.

Stir in remaining ingredients, combining thoroughly. With a small-portion scoop, drop mounds of batter 2 inches apart on baking sheets; or lightly flour hands and roll dough into 40 balls, each about 1 tablespoon, and place on baking sheets.

Bake for about 16 minutes, or just until lightly browned around edges. Transfer cookies to cooling rack and let cool completely.

COOK'S TIP ON DOUGH SCOOPS: You can simplify cookie baking by using dough scoops to portion the dough. The scoops look and function like the kind of ice cream scoop that uses a quick-release lever. Available at gourmet shops, the scoops come in sizes to make cookies from dainty to jumbo.

Calories 170
Protein 3 g
Carbohydrates 29 g
Fiber 2 g
Total Fat 5 g
  Saturated 0 g
  Polyunsaturated 1 g
  Monounsaturated 3 g
Cholesterol 0 mg
Sodium 9 mg

oatmeal lace cookies

SERVES 15; 2 COOKIES PER SERVING

You can leave these delicate cookies flat or, while they're still warm, easily shape them into a "U," then overlap them on a serving dish for an interesting presentation.

Vegetable oil spray
1/2 cup firmly packed light brown sugar
1/4 cup sugar
3 tablespoons acceptable vegetable oil
2 tablespoons dark corn syrup
White of 1 large egg
1 tablespoon water

1/2 teaspoon vanilla extract
1/4 teaspoon almond extract
1 cup rolled oats, uncooked
2 tablespoons all-purpose flour
1/4 teaspoon baking soda
1/4 teaspoon salt

Preheat oven to 350°F. Line two baking sheets with cooking parchment, and spray with vegetable oil spray.

In a large mixing bowl, beat sugars, oil, and corn syrup with an electric mixer on medium until combined.

Add egg white, water, and extracts; beat until smooth.

Stir in oats.

In a small bowl, combine remaining ingredients. Add to oat mixture, stirring until well blended.

Drop dough by rounded teaspoonfuls 3 inches apart on baking sheets. With a spoon or fork dipped in water, flatten each cookie into a 1 1/2-inch circle.

Bake for 6 to 8 minutes, or until lightly browned, watching carefully. Let cool on cooking parchment until slightly warm; using a pancake turner or spatula, remove cookies from cooking parchment. For flat cookies, let cool completely on cooling rack. If curved cookies are desired, drape slightly warm cookies over a rounded form, such as a narrow rolling pin or the handle of a wooden spoon set across two cups and let cool completely. Freeze leftover cookies in an airtight container. (In warm, humid weather, they quickly pick up moisture from the air.)

COOK'S TIP: If these cookies are underbaked, they will be sticky. However, be careful not to overbake, or they will scorch and be very chewy. The cooking parchment makes it easy to remove the cookies from the baking sheets.

Calories 99
Protein 2 g
Carbohydrates 17 g
Fiber 1 g
Total Fat 3 g
  Saturated 0 g
  Polyunsaturated 2 g
  Monounsaturated 1 g
Cholesterol 0 mg
Sodium 71 mg

low-fat & luscious desserts

brandy orange snaps

These snappy cookies are fun to watch while they bake. They bubble and spread out, creating a lacy pattern. They are great as a finishing touch to an elegant dessert or with your favorite warm beverage.

Vegetable oil spray (optional)
⅓ cup light corn syrup
¼ cup sugar
2 tablespoons light stick margarine
2 tablespoons brandy or orange juice

2 teaspoons molasses
1 teaspoon ground ginger
1 teaspoon grated orange zest
½ cup all-purpose flour

Preheat oven to 350°F. Line a large baking sheet with cooking parchment, or spray with vegetable oil spray.

In a medium saucepan, whisk together all ingredients except flour; cook over medium heat until margarine has melted and sugar has dissolved, 2 to 3 minutes, whisking occasionally. Remove from heat and let cool slightly for 2 minutes.

Stir in flour (batter will be slightly lumpy). Let sit for about 5 minutes so batter will thicken slightly.

Spoon six mounds of batter by heaping teaspoonfuls about 3 inches apart on baking sheet.

Bake for 10 minutes, or until cookies have spread out and are golden brown. For flat cookies, let cookies cool on cooking parchment for 5 minutes; transfer to a cooling rack. For "U"–shaped cookies, let cookies cool on cooking parchment for about 3 minutes; using a flexible metal spatula, remove cookies and shape them over a rounded form, such as a narrow rolling pin or the handle of a wooden spoon set across two cups to form a curve; let cool completely. Transfer to a cooling rack. Store cookies in an airtight container.

COOK'S TIP: Although you can fit more cookies on a baking sheet, we recommend baking only six cookies at a time. That way, once you begin to shape the cookies, you'll have time to complete that step before they stick to the parchment.

Calories 55
Protein 1 g
Carbohydrates 11 g
Fiber 0 g
Total Fat 1 g
  Saturated 0 g
  Polyunsaturated 0 g
  Monounsaturated 0 g
Cholesterol 0 mg
Sodium 17 mg

drop sugar cookies

These holiday cookies are perfect for company. Let the children help by sprinkling a variety of colored sugars over the big, soft cookies for festive results.

Vegetable oil spray (optional)
2 cups sugar
⅔ cup light tub margarine, softened
2 tablespoons vanilla extract
Egg substitute equivalent to 2 eggs, or 2 large eggs

3 cups all-purpose flour
1 teaspoon baking soda
¼ teaspoon salt
½ cup fat-free milk
½ cup colored sugars

Preheat oven to 400°F. Line two baking sheets with cooking parchment, or spray baking sheets with vegetable oil spray. Set aside.

In a large mixing bowl, combine sugar, margarine, and vanilla.

Add egg substitute; beat with an electric mixer on medium until well blended.

In a large bowl, combine flour, baking soda, and salt; gradually stir into sugar mixture, blending until smooth.

Blend in milk.

Drop mounds of dough, about 2 tablespoons each, onto baking sheets. (A small-portion scoop [see Cook's Tip on Dough Scoops, page 35] works well for this.) Moisten palm of your hand and slightly flatten each cookie to about 2 inches in diameter. Sprinkle with colored sugars.

Bake for 8 minutes, or until edges are lightly brown. Transfer cookies, still on cooking parchment, to cooling racks; let cookies cool completely.

Calories 247
Protein 3 g
Carbohydrates 51 g
Fiber 1 g
Total Fat 3 g
  Saturated 1 g
  Polyunsaturated 1 g
  Monounsaturated 1 g
Cholesterol 0 mg
Sodium 182 mg

frosted pineapple cookies

Crushed pineapple contributes moistness and a mild flavor to these irresistible, very easy to make cookies. For the best results, freeze them until a few minutes before serving time.

Vegetable oil spray (optional)

cookies

- 1   8-ounce can crushed pineapple in its own juice, very well drained (reserve liquid)
- ½   cup firmly packed light brown sugar
- ½   cup sugar
  Egg substitute equivalent to 1 egg, or 1 large egg, beaten
- 2   tablespoons acceptable vegetable oil
- 1   teaspoon vanilla extract

- 1   cup all-purpose flour
- 1   teaspoon baking powder
- ½   teaspoon baking soda
- ¼   teaspoon salt
- 1⅓   cups rolled oats, uncooked

glaze

- ⅔   cup sifted confectioners' sugar
- 1   tablespoon plus 1 teaspoon reserved pineapple juice
  Pinch of salt

Preheat oven to 350°F. Line two baking sheets with cooking parchment, or spray with vegetable oil spray.

For cookies, in a large bowl, stir together pineapple, sugars, egg substitute, oil, and vanilla.

In a small bowl, stir together remaining cookie ingredients except rolled oats. Add to pineapple mixture, stirring until smooth.

Stir in rolled oats. Drop mixture by rounded teaspoonfuls 2 inches apart onto baking sheets.

Bake for 10 to 12 minutes, or until very lightly browned. Slide cookies, still on cooking parchment, onto countertop and let cool slightly; if not using cooking parchment, transfer cookies onto a cooling rack to cool slightly.

In a small bowl, whisk together glaze ingredients. Spread or drizzle over warm cookies. Let cookies cool completely, then freeze in an airtight container. To serve, place cookies on a serving tray and let them thaw for a few minutes.

COOK'S TIP: One way to thoroughly drain canned pineapple is to put it in a colander, then use a spoon to press on the fruit and extract even more liquid.

Calories 133
Protein 2 g
Carbohydrates 27 g
Fiber 1 g
Total Fat 2 g
 Saturated 0 g
 Polyunsaturated 1 g
 Monounsaturated 1 g
Cholesterol 0 mg
Sodium 111 mg

butterscotchers

These chewy, buttery-tasting cookies with bits of butterscotch are delicious straight from the oven or up to three days old—if they last that long!

¼ cup acceptable stick margarine, softened
⅓ cup firmly packed dark brown sugar
⅓ cup sugar
   Egg substitute equivalent to 1 egg, or whites of 2 large eggs
1 teaspoon vanilla, butter, and nut flavoring or vanilla extract

1 cup plus 2 tablespoons all-purpose flour
½ teaspoon ground cinnamon
½ teaspoon baking soda
¼ teaspoon salt
½ cup butterscotch morsels

Preheat oven to 350°F.

In a medium mixing bowl, with an electric mixer on low, beat margarine until smooth.

Add sugars; beat until well blended.

Add egg substitute and vanilla, butter, and nut flavoring; beat until smooth.

Add remaining ingredients except butterscotch morsels; beat until well blended.

Stir in butterscotch morsels.

On two nonstick baking sheets or baking sheets lined with cooking parchment, drop batter by rounded teaspoonfuls 2 inches apart (12 cookies on a baking sheet); set one baking sheet aside.

Bake cookies on other baking sheet for 9 minutes (cookies won't look quite done). Let cookies stand on baking sheet for 1 full minute to finish cooking without drying out. Transfer cookies to a cooling rack immediately so they won't stick to baking sheet; let cool completely.

Meanwhile, bake cookies on second baking sheet.

Calories 81
Protein 1 g
Carbohydrates 13 g
Fiber 0 g
Total Fat 3 g
  Saturated 1 g
  Polyunsaturated 1 g
  Monounsaturated 1 g
Cholesterol 0 mg
Sodium 82 mg

pumpkin nutmeg cookies

SERVES 24; 2 COOKIES PER SERVING

All the flavors of a great pumpkin pie enhance these cookies.

2 1/2   cups all-purpose flour
2   teaspoons ground cinnamon
2   teaspoons ground nutmeg
1   teaspoon baking powder
1   teaspoon baking soda
1/2   teaspoon salt
1 1/2   cups sugar
1/2   cup light stick margarine, softened

Egg substitute equivalent to 1 egg, or 1 large egg
1   cup solid-pack canned pumpkin (not pie filling)
1   teaspoon vanilla extract
1   cup chopped pecans, dry-roasted (see Cook's Tip on Dry-Roasting Nuts, page 68)

Preheat oven to 350°F. Line two baking sheets with cooking parchment. Set aside.

In a large bowl, sift together flour, cinnamon, nutmeg, baking powder, baking soda, and salt. Set aside.

In a large mixing bowl, using an electric mixer on medium, cream sugar and margarine for 3 minutes.

With mixer running, gradually beat in egg substitute.

Beat in pumpkin and vanilla.

Gradually add flour mixture to pumpkin mixture, beating well after each addition.

Stir in pecans. Drop dough by heaping teaspoonfuls about 2 inches apart on baking sheets.

Bake for 12 to 15 minutes, or until light brown. Let cookies cool completely on baking sheets.

Calories 151
Protein 2 g
Carbohydrates 25 g
Fiber 1 g
Total Fat 5 g
  Saturated 1 g
  Polyunsaturated 2 g
  Monounsaturated 1 g
Cholesterol 0 mg
Sodium 150 mg

ginger nut cookies

The perfect accompaniment for tea, coffee, and spiced cider, this cookie is nutty, soft, and chewy. If you're a true ginger-lover, use the larger measurement of crystallized ginger and chop it coarsely. When you bite into a piece of it, you'll get that zing that only ginger provides.

Vegetable oil spray
2/3 cup sugar
2/3 cup firmly packed light brown sugar
6 tablespoons light stick margarine, softened
2 teaspoons vanilla extract
2 large eggs (not egg substitute)

1 3/4 cups all-purpose flour
3/4 teaspoon baking soda
1/4 teaspoon salt
1/2 to 3/4 cup finely or coarsely chopped crystallized ginger (3 to 4 1/2 ounces)
1/2 cup coarsely chopped pecans

Preheat oven to 350°F. Spray two baking sheets with vegetable oil spray, or line with cooking parchment.

In a large mixing bowl, using an electric mixer on medium, cream sugars and margarine until fluffy, about 3 minutes.

Add vanilla and beat thoroughly.

Add eggs, one at a time, beating after each addition.

In a medium bowl, sift together flour, baking soda, and salt. Gradually add to margarine mixture, beating after each addition until well mixed.

Add ginger and pecans, stirring only to combine. Using a tablespoon or small-portion scoop, drop mounds of batter 2 inches apart on baking sheets.

Bake for 10 to 12 minutes, or until lightly browned. Put baking sheets on cooling racks and let cookies cool for 3 to 5 minutes; remove cookies from baking sheets and let cool completely on cooling racks.

COOK'S TIP ON CRYSTALLIZED GINGER: Crystallized, or candied, ginger is cooked in a sugar syrup, then coated with sugar. To chop or mince slices of crystallized ginger, pulse them on and off in a food processor or mini-processor. It may help to lightly spray the blade with vegetable oil spray before beginning. If the ginger starts to clump as you chop it, add a little sugar and continue to pulse. Another option is to grate the crystallized ginger with a rasp made specifically to use with food.

Calories 159
Protein 2 g
Carbohydrates 30 g
Fiber 1 g
Total Fat 4 g
  Saturated 1 g
  Polyunsaturated 1 g
  Monounsaturated 2 g
Cholesterol 21 mg
Sodium 107 mg

cherry oat cookies

SERVES 36; 2 COOKIES PER SERVING

Soft and chewy, these cherry cookies are perfect for a breakfast treat with a tall glass of fat-free milk, at teatime, or for a snack.

2 1/4 cups dried cherries, dried cranberries, or dried blueberries, or a combination

1 1/2 cups water

2 cups all-purpose flour

1 1/2 teaspoons ground cinnamon

3/4 teaspoon baking soda

1/4 cup plus 2 tablespoons light tub margarine

2 tablespoons acceptable vegetable oil

1 cup firmly packed dark brown sugar

1 1/2 teaspoons vanilla extract

Whites of 3 large eggs

1 1/2 cups rolled oats, uncooked

3/4 cup oat bran, uncooked

Preheat oven to 375°F.

In a small, heavy saucepan, bring cherries and water to a boil over medium-high heat; boil for 4 to 6 minutes, or until cherries are plump, stirring occasionally. Drain cherries, reserving 5 tablespoons liquid; set both aside.

In a medium bowl, sift together flour, cinnamon, and baking soda. Set aside.

In a large mixing bowl, with an electric mixer, cream margarine and oil.

Add brown sugar and vanilla, beating until light in color, about 1 minute.

Add egg whites and beat until smooth, occasionally scraping bowl with a rubber scraper.

Add reserved cherry liquid, beating until well mixed.

Reduce speed to low and gradually add flour mixture with mixer running.

Add rolled oats, oat bran, and cherries, stirring just until incorporated. Using a small-portion scoop or tablespoon, drop cookie dough onto heavy ungreased baking sheets or regular baking sheets lined with cooking parchment, leaving about 1 inch between cookies.

Bake for 15 minutes. Transfer cookies from baking sheets to cooling racks and let cool completely, about 20 minutes.

Calories 99
Protein 2 g
Carbohydrates 21 g
Fiber 1 g
Total Fat 2 g
  Saturated 0 g
  Polyunsaturated 1 g
  Monounsaturated 1 g
Cholesterol 0 mg
Sodium 49 mg

gingerbread window cookies

SERVES 20; 2 3¹/₂-INCH COOKIES PER SERVING

We hope these cookies will become a tradition in your household.
They are especially fun for kids—of all ages—to prepare.

2¹/₂ cups all-purpose flour
1 teaspoon ground ginger
¹/₂ teaspoon ground cinnamon
¹/₂ teaspoon ground cloves
¹/₂ teaspoon baking soda
¹/₂ cup sugar
¹/₄ cup light margarine, softened
¹/₃ cup molasses
Egg substitute equivalent to 1 egg,
or 1 large egg

2 tablespoons unsweetened applesauce
1 tablespoon vinegar
30 pieces assorted hard candies, such as fruit flavored, cinnamon, butterscotch, or sour balls
Vegetable oil spray
Flour for rolling out dough

In a medium bowl, stir together 2¹/₂ cups flour, ginger, cinnamon, cloves, and baking soda. Set aside.

In a large mixing bowl, cream sugar and margarine with an electric mixer on medium.

Beat in molasses, egg substitute, applesauce, and vinegar.

Gradually add flour mixture, beating after each addition. Divide dough in half; shape each piece into a disk. Wrap dough in plastic wrap and refrigerate for 2 hours to two days.

Meanwhile, sort candies by color if using fruit flavored or sour balls, unwrap them, and put candies of each color in a separate airtight freezer bag. Seal bags and place on a flat surface, such as a cutting board. Using flat side of a meat mallet or a clean hammer, crush candies into small pieces (not into powder). Keep crushed candies in airtight bags until ready to use.

Preheat oven to 350°F. Line four baking sheets with aluminum foil; spray foil with vegetable oil spray.

Lightly flour a flat surface. Roll one chilled dough disk to ¹/₄-inch thickness. Cut out your favorite shapes (3¹/₂-inch cutters make about 40 cookies), such as hearts for Valentine's Day. Place cookies about 1 inch apart on baking sheets. Using a smaller cookie cutter (circular cutters ³/₄ to 1 inch in diameter work well), cut a shape out of center of each cookie, cutting all the way through dough. Remove cutouts. Lightly place small cookie cutter back where you cut out dough. Spoon about 1¹/₂ teaspoons crushed hard candies over area within small

Calories 139
Protein 2 g
Carbohydrates 30 g
Fiber 1 g
Total Fat 1 g
  Saturated 0 g
  Polyunsaturated 0 g
  Monounsaturated 0 g
Cholesterol 0 mg
Sodium 59 mg

low-fat & luscious desserts

cookie cutter. Remove cookie cutter (candies should mound slightly above the cutout). Repeat with remaining dough and candies. (Dough scraps can be mounded together and rerolled.)

Bake for 6 to 9 minutes, or until cookies are firm but tender and candies have melted. Let cool on cooling racks for 15 minutes. Refrigerate leftover cookies in an airtight container for up to one week, separating layers of cookies with wax paper.

trail mix squares

Wrap these cookie squares in colored plastic wrap and take them on the road (or trail!) or to school for a lunch box treat. Use only one type of dried fruit or put together a combination of your favorites.

Vegetable oil spray
2 cups large marshmallows (about 16)
1 tablespoon light stick margarine
2 tablespoons unsalted sunflower seeds
2 tablespoons toasted wheat germ (honey-nut flavor preferred)

1 1/2 cups puffed wheat cereal
1 cup crisp rice cereal
1 cup chopped dried fruit, such as apricots, pears, prunes, apples, or dried cranberries, or whole golden raisins

Spray a medium microwave-safe bowl, a large bowl, and an 8-inch square cake pan with vegetable oil spray.

In medium bowl, microwave marshmallows and margarine on 100 percent power (high), uncovered, for 30 to 60 seconds, or until marshmallows are melted, stirring after 30 seconds if more melting is needed.

Stir in sunflower seeds and wheat germ (mixture will be very thick).

In a large bowl, combine remaining ingredients; stir in marshmallow mixture. Spoon into cake pan; place a piece of plastic wrap over mixture and press to distribute mixture evenly (plastic wrap keeps mixture from sticking to your hands). Discard plastic wrap. Let mixture stand for 30 minutes, then cut into 2-inch squares. Squares can be stored in an airtight container for up to five days.

Calories 66
Protein 1 g
Carbohydrates 14 g
Fiber 1 g
Total Fat 1 g
  Saturated 0 g
  Polyunsaturated 1 g
  Monounsaturated 0 g
Cholesterol 0 mg
Sodium 27 mg

lemon-date bars

Thanks to the convenience of date bread mix, these tangy cookies take only minutes to prepare.

Vegetable oil spray

crust

1 1-pound 6-ounce box date bread mix with real dates

1/3 cup light tub margarine or light stick margarine, cut into chunks

Egg substitute equivalent to 1 egg

filling

Egg substitute equivalent to 4 eggs

3/4 cup sugar

2 teaspoons grated lemon zest

1/4 cup fresh lemon juice

2 tablespoons confectioners' sugar

Preheat oven to 350°F. Spray a 13 × 9 × 2-inch baking pan with vegetable oil spray.

For crust, in a medium bowl, blend date bread mix and margarine with a pastry blender, two knives, or a fork until crumbly.

Add egg substitute; blend well. Press mixture firmly over bottom of pan.

Bake for 12 minutes.

Meanwhile, put filling ingredients in a food processor or medium mixing bowl. Process or beat for 30 seconds. Pour over hot crust.

Bake for 15 to 20 minutes, or until center is set and edges are golden brown. Let cool completely on a cooling rack. Cut into 24 bars.

Using a strainer, shake confectioners' sugar evenly over bars. Bars can be frozen for up to 3 months, defrosted at room temperature, and sprinkled with additional confectioners' sugar before serving.

Calories 142
Protein 3 g
Carbohydrates 29 g
Fiber 1 g
Total Fat 2 g
  Saturated 0 g
  Polyunsaturated 0 g
  Monounsaturated 1 g
Cholesterol 0 mg
Sodium 141 mg

lemony lime squares

A double dose of citrus goes into a cherished classic. Though these bars require a lot of ingredients, they are easy to prepare.

Vegetable oil spray
1 cup all-purpose flour
1/4 cup sugar
1/4 cup chopped pecans
1/4 cup light stick margarine, cut into 4 pieces
2/3 cup sugar
Whites of 2 large eggs
Egg substitute equivalent to 1 egg, or 1 large egg

2 tablespoons all-purpose flour
1/2 teaspoon grated lemon zest
3 tablespoons fresh lemon juice
1/2 teaspoon grated lime zest
3 tablespoons fresh lime juice (about 2 medium limes)
1/2 teaspoon baking powder
2 tablespoons confectioners' sugar

Preheat oven to 350°F. Spray an 8-inch square baking dish with vegetable oil spray.

In a medium mixing bowl, combine flour, 1/4 cup sugar, pecans, and margarine; beat with an electric mixer on medium until mixture is crumbly. Press evenly on bottom of baking dish.

Bake for 15 minutes.

Meanwhile, in same bowl, beat remaining ingredients except confectioners' sugar on medium for about 2 minutes (mixture will be thin). Pour over hot crust.

Bake for 20 to 23 minutes, or until topping is set (mixture doesn't jiggle when gently shaken). Let cool on a cooling rack for 30 minutes before cutting into squares. Dust with confectioners' sugar just before serving.

Calories 111
Protein 2 g
Carbohydrates 20 g
Fiber 0 g
Total Fat 3 g
  Saturated 0 g
  Polyunsaturated 1 g
  Monounsaturated 1 g
Cholesterol 0 mg
Sodium 49 mg

raspberry blondies

SERVES 16; 1 BAR PER SERVING

Raspberries turn these bar cookies into a special treat.
Raspberry all-fruit spread makes them even better.

Vegetable oil spray
½ cup light stick margarine
2¾ cups all-purpose flour
½ teaspoon baking soda
¼ teaspoon salt
2 cups sugar

Egg substitute equivalent to 4 eggs
2 teaspoons vanilla extract
1 cup frozen lightly sweetened raspberries
1 10-ounce jar raspberry all-fruit spread (optional)

Preheat oven to 350°F. Spray a 13 × 9 × 2-inch baking pan with vegetable oil spray. Set aside.

In a small saucepan, melt margarine; set aside to cool.

In a medium bowl, sift together flour, baking soda, and salt.

In a large bowl, whisk together sugar and egg substitute, then whisk in vanilla and margarine.

Using a spoon, stir flour mixture into sugar mixture.

Carefully fold in raspberries (mixture will be stiff). Pour mixture into baking pan.

Bake for 25 to 30 minutes, or until a toothpick inserted in center comes out with a moist crumb. Let cool on a cooling rack for about 15 minutes before cutting into 16 bars.

In a small saucepan, heat all-fruit spread over low heat for about 5 minutes, or until melted, whisking occasionally. Pour over each bar.

RASPBERRY BROWNIES

Follow directions above, reducing flour to 2 cups. When margarine has melted, remove from heat and whisk in ⅔ cup unsweetened cocoa powder. Let stand for 10 minutes, then whisk into sugar mixture. Continue as directed above.

COOK'S TIP: Adding the raspberry all-fruit spread doesn't change the amount of fat or cholesterol, but it does increase the calorie count by about 3 percent.

RASPBERRY BLONDIES

Calories 214
Protein 4 g
Carbohydrates 43 g
Fiber 1 g
Total Fat 3 g
  Saturated 1 g
  Polyunsaturated 1 g
  Monounsaturated 1 g
Cholesterol 0 mg
Sodium 145 mg

RASPBERRY BROWNIES

Calories 201
Protein 4 g
Carbohydrates 41 g
Fiber 2 g
Total Fat 3 g
  Saturated 1 g
  Polyunsaturated 1 g
  Monounsaturated 1 g
Cholesterol 0 mg
Sodium 146 mg

Bourbon Street Pecan Pie

Mango Coconut Cream Pie

Granola Bar Pie with Pretzel Crust

Key Lime Pie

Banana Cream Pie

Frozen Pumpkin Pie with Gingersnap Crust

Frozen Turtle Pie

Tropical Fruit Pie

Lighter-Than-Air Lemon Pie

Cherry Berry Pie

Summertime Peach Tart

Mixed Berry Tart with Apricot Glaze

Fruit Platter Tart

Cinnamon-Scented Pear Crisp

Home-Style Blackberry Cobbler

Home-Style Peach Cobbler

Skillet Cherry Crumble

Ricotta Pie with Cassis Berries

Ricotta Pie with Chocolate Syrup

Vanilla Apples in Phyllo Nests

Basic Piecrust

perfect
pies

bourbon street pecan pie

*You can almost hear the jazz on Bourbon Street when you bite into this pie.
Serve it around the holidays and for a heart-healthy Mardi Gras celebration!*

Vegetable oil spray

crust

1½ cups reduced-fat graham cracker crumbs
   (about 24 squares)
3 tablespoons fresh orange juice
¼ teaspoon ground nutmeg

filling

1 cup firmly packed light brown sugar
1 cup dark corn syrup
   Egg substitute equivalent to 3 eggs
2 tablespoons bourbon or 1 teaspoon rum
   extract
1 tablespoon light stick margarine, melted
1 teaspoon grated orange zest
⅛ teaspoon salt
⅓ cup chopped pecans

Preheat oven to 350°F. Spray a 9-inch pie pan with vegetable oil spray.

For crust, in a small bowl, combine all ingredients with a fork or
spoon. Pour mixture into pie pan. Place a piece of plastic wrap over
the crumb mixture and press with your hands to spread mixture
evenly over bottom and up sides of pie pan (plastic will prevent
crumbs from sticking to your hands). Discard plastic wrap.

For filling, in a medium bowl, combine all ingredients except pecans.
Pour into pie shell; sprinkle with pecans. Cover edge of crust with aluminum foil to keep it from burning.

Place pie on a rimmed baking sheet; bake for 25 minutes. Remove foil
and bake for 25 minutes, or until set (center doesn't jiggle when pie is
gently shaken). Let pie cool on cooling rack for 1 hour before serving.

Calories 342
Protein 4 g
Carbohydrates 73 g
Fiber 1 g
Total Fat 5 g
  Saturated 0 g
  Polyunsaturated 1 g
  Monounsaturated 3 g
Cholesterol 0 mg
Sodium 223 mg

mango coconut cream pie

SERVES 8

Mango slices adorn a custardlike filling flavored with white chocolate and coconut in this fitting finale for an outdoor party.

Vegetable oil spray
3/4 cup reduced-fat vanilla wafer crumbs (about 21 wafers)
3/4 cup reduced-fat graham cracker crumbs (about 12 squares)
2 tablespoons orange juice
2 tablespoons unsweetened applesauce
1 small package sugar-free, fat-free (about 1 ounce) or regular (about 3.4 ounces) instant white chocolate or vanilla pudding mix
1 3/4 cups fat-free milk

2 cups frozen fat-free or light whipped topping, thawed (about 5 ounces)
2 tablespoons shredded sweetened coconut
2 tablespoons coconut-flavored rum or 1/2 teaspoon rum extract (optional)
1 teaspoon coconut extract
1 large mango, peeled and thinly sliced (about 1 1/2 cups)
1 tablespoon sweetened shredded coconut, toasted (optional)

Preheat oven to 350°F. Spray a 9-inch pie pan with vegetable oil spray.

In a medium bowl, stir together vanilla wafer and graham cracker crumbs, orange juice, and applesauce; transfer to pie pan. Place a piece of plastic wrap over the crumb mixture and press with your hands to spread mixture evenly over bottom and up sides of pie pan (plastic will prevent crumbs from sticking to your hands). Discard plastic wrap.

Bake for 10 minutes. Let cool on a cooling rack for 15 to 20 minutes.

Meanwhile, prepare pudding according to package directions but using 1 3/4 cups fat-free milk.

Stir in whipped topping, 2 tablespoons coconut, coconut rum, and coconut extract. Spread evenly in piecrust.

Arrange mango slices in a decorative pattern on pie; sprinkle with toasted coconut. Refrigerate for at least 1 hour before slicing.

COOK'S TIP ON TOASTING COCONUT: To toast, spread the coconut in a single layer on a baking sheet. Bake at 325°F for 5 to 6 minutes, or until lightly toasted, stirring occasionally.

Calories 162
Protein 3 g
Carbohydrates 32 g
Fiber 1 g
Total Fat 2 g
 Saturated 1 g
 Polyunsaturated 0 g
 Monounsaturated 0 g
Cholesterol 1 mg
Sodium 255 mg

granola bar pie
with pretzel crust

This rich, chewy pie filled with granola bar ingredients is a winner with kids and adults alike.

Vegetable oil spray

crust

2 cups crushed unsalted pretzels (about 7 ounces)

Whites of 3 large eggs, beaten with a fork

1 tablespoon light stick margarine, melted

filling

Whites of 4 large eggs

1 large egg, or egg substitute equivalent to 1 egg

2 tablespoons light tub margarine, melted

3/4 cup frozen fat-free or light whipped topping, thawed

2/3 cup rolled oats, uncooked

1/2 cup sugar

1/2 cup firmly packed light brown sugar

1/2 cup dried cranberries

1/2 cup dark corn syrup

1/4 cup sweetened shredded coconut

3 tablespoons chopped or sliced almonds

3 tablespoons chopped walnuts

1 1/2 teaspoons vanilla extract

❖

1 to 2 tablespoons confectioners' sugar for dusting (optional)

Dried cranberries (optional)

Preheat oven to 425°F. Spray a 10-inch glass pie pan with vegetable oil spray.

For crust, in a small bowl, combine all ingredients. With fingertips, firmly press mixture on bottom and up sides of pie pan.

For filling, in a large bowl, whisk together egg whites and egg until frothy.

Whisk in margarine.

Add remaining filling ingredients, stirring well. Pour into crust.

Bake for 55 to 60 minutes, or until filling is set and a toothpick inserted in center comes out clean. Let cool completely, at least 1 hour, on a cooling rack.

If desired, place stencil(s) on pie and dust with confectioners' sugar; carefully remove stencil(s) to reveal design. If you prefer, sift confectioners' sugar over top of pie without using stencil(s). Garnish with dried cranberries.

COOK'S TIP ON CONFECTIONERS' SUGAR: For even distribution, use a fine-mesh strainer to sprinkle confectioners' sugar.

Calories 271
Protein 6 g
Carbohydrates 51 g
Fiber 2 g
Total Fat 5 g
  Saturated 1 g
  Polyunsaturated 2 g
  Monounsaturated 2 g
Cholesterol 18 mg
Sodium 136 mg

low-fat & luscious desserts

key lime pie

SERVES 8

This light, refreshing, and mildly tart version of Key lime pie is best served frozen. You can spoon additional whipped topping on the finished pie just before serving for an extra dollop of pleasure.

crust

- 1¼ cups low-fat graham cracker crumbs (about 20 squares)
- 3 tablespoons light stick margarine, melted
- 2 tablespoons sugar (optional)

filling

- 1 14-ounce can fat-free sweetened condensed milk
- ½ teaspoon finely grated lime zest
- ½ cup fresh Key lime juice or fresh lime juice (10 to 12 Key limes or about 8 medium limes)
- 16 ounces fat-free or light frozen whipped topping, thawed for about 1 hour at room temperature (about 6 cups)

❖

Fat-free or light frozen whipped topping, thawed (optional)
Finely grated lime zest (optional)

Preheat oven to 375°F.

For crust, in a medium bowl, stir together all ingredients. Press on bottom and up sides of a 9-inch pie pan.

Bake for 6 minutes. Let cool completely on a cooling rack.

For filling, in a large bowl, whisk together all ingredients except whipped topping.

Using a rubber spatula, gently fold in partially thawed whipped topping until blended. Spoon into cooled crust. Using back of a spoon, make swirling motions to form a decorative top. Cover loosely with plastic wrap and freeze until firm, about 1 hour. If you prefer a puddinglike consistency, refrigerate pie until thoroughly chilled instead of freezing.

To serve, top each slice with a dollop of whipped topping and a sprinkle of lime zest.

COOK'S TIP: Baking the graham cracker crust creates a crisp, almost nutty texture, but you can skip this step if you wish. For an unbaked crust, press the mixture on the bottom and up the sides of the pie pan; chill for 30 minutes before filling.

COOK'S TIP ON KEY LIMES: Smaller and rounder than the more readily available Persian limes, Key limes have a higher acid content and are yellower in color. If you can't find fresh Key limes, look for bottles of juice near the bottled lemon and lime juice in most supermarkets.

Calories 325
Protein 5 g
Carbohydrates 65 g
Fiber 1 g
Total Fat 3 g
  Saturated 0 g
  Polyunsaturated 1 g
  Monounsaturated 1 g
Cholesterol 3 mg
Sodium 184 mg

banana cream pie

Supremely elegant and wonderfully creamy, this pie looks and tastes as decadent as the original version. Thanks to fat-free dairy products, you can easily create this classic dessert without the notorious calories and fat.

crust
- 40 reduced-fat vanilla wafers
- 3 tablespoons light tub margarine, melted

filling
- 1 1/2 cups fat-free milk
- 1 14-ounce can fat-free sweetened condensed milk
  Egg substitute equivalent to 1 egg, or 1 large egg
- 1/3 cup all-purpose flour
- 2 1/2 cups thinly sliced ripe, firm bananas (about 3 medium)
- 2 teaspoons vanilla extract

meringue
  Whites of 4 large eggs, room temperature
- 1/4 cup sugar

Preheat oven to 325°F.

For crust, in a food processor or blender, process vanilla wafers until finely crushed (or place vanilla wafers in an airtight plastic bag and crush with a rolling pin).

Add margarine and process until well blended. Press mixture on bottom and up sides of a 9-inch pie pan.

For filling, in a medium saucepan, whisk together milk, condensed milk, and egg substitute.

Gradually whisk in flour. Cook over medium heat for 6 to 8 minutes, or until thick, whisking constantly. Remove from heat.

Fold in bananas and vanilla. Spoon into crust.

For meringue, in a large mixing bowl, beat egg whites with an electric mixer on high until foamy.

Add sugar, 1 to 2 tablespoons at a time, beating after each addition until stiff, glossy peaks form. (Peaks shouldn't fold over when beater is lifted, and meringue shouldn't feel gritty when rubbed between fingers.) Spoon meringue over banana mixture; using back of a spoon, make swirling motions to form a decorative design on meringue.

Bake for 20 minutes, or until meringue is golden. Let cool on a cooling rack for 30 minutes before serving (to allow filling to become firm). Loosely wrapped in plastic wrap, pie will keep for up to 24 hours in refrigerator. (After that, bananas begin to brown.)

Calories 355
Protein 10 g
Carbohydrates 71 g
Fiber 1 g
Total Fat 3 g
 Saturated 1 g
 Polyunsaturated 1 g
 Monounsaturated 1 g
Cholesterol 4 mg
Sodium 215 mg

frozen pumpkin pie with gingersnap crust

SERVES 10

Start a new Thanksgiving tradition by serving this frozen version of the classic, featuring a gingersnap crust for zippy flavor.

crust

- 16 reduced-fat gingersnap cookies
- 1 tablespoon light stick margarine, melted

filling

- 1 quart vanilla nonfat or low-fat frozen yogurt or ice milk, softened
- 7/8 cup canned solid-pack pumpkin (not pie filling) (about 1/2 15-ounce can)
- 1/2 teaspoon ground cinnamon
- 1/2 teaspoon ground ginger
- 1/4 teaspoon ground nutmeg
- 1/8 teaspoon ground cloves

Preheat oven to 300°F.

For crust, in a food processor or blender, process cookies into fine crumbs.

Slowly add margarine, processing until well combined. Remove 1 tablespoon crumb mixture. Set aside. Press remaining mixture onto bottom and up sides of a 9-inch pie pan.

Bake for 15 minutes. Let cool on a cooling rack.

Meanwhile, in a large bowl, beat filling ingredients with an electric mixer until well combined. Spoon into cooled crust. Sprinkle with reserved crumbs. Cover with plastic wrap and freeze for 4 hours, or until firm.

Calories 136
Protein 5 g
Carbohydrates 26 g
Fiber 1 g
Total Fat 2 g
  Saturated 1 g
  Polyunsaturated 0 g
  Monounsaturated 1 g
Cholesterol 1 mg
Sodium 133 mg

frozen turtle pie

Reminiscent of turtle candies, this pie combines a crust of chocolate-flavor vanilla wafers with ice cream, caramel sauce, pecans, and a drizzle of chocolate. You can make part of this delicious dessert up to a week ahead, or prepare the whole thing a day ahead and freeze it. If you want to make it the day you serve it, be sure to start early enough for the various freezing steps.

Vegetable oil spray

chocolate crumb crust

36 reduced-fat chocolate-flavor vanilla wafers, coarsely crumbled by hand

3 tablespoons light stick margarine, melted

caramel sauce

1 cup sugar

½ cup water

¾ cup fat-free evaporated milk, room temperature

1 teaspoon vanilla extract

❖

1 quart nonfat ice cream or frozen yogurt, such as vanilla or coffee

2 ounces reduced-fat semisweet chocolate chips, finely chopped, or 2 tablespoons fat-free chocolate syrup (optional)

¼ cup chopped dry-roasted pecans (see Cook's Tip on Dry-Roasting Nuts, page 68)

Preheat oven to 350°F. Spray a 9-inch deep-dish glass pie pan with vegetable oil spray.

For crust, in a food processor, pulse cookies until finely ground.

Pour margarine through feed tube, pulsing on and off until combined. Pat into pie pan, spreading evenly on bottom and sides.

Bake for about 10 minutes, or until dry. Let cool completely on a cooling rack, about 30 minutes.

For caramel sauce, in a medium, heavy-bottom saucepan, stir together sugar and water. Bring to a boil over medium heat, swirling pan gently once or twice, until sugar is a medium amber color or registers 300°F on a candy thermometer or instant-read thermometer. Be careful, because once caramel begins to color, it will darken very quickly. Immediately remove from heat when desired color is reached. Let cool for 1 minute.

Gently whisk in evaporated milk. If mixture forms a ball, or "seizes," put pan over medium heat and stir until mixture has dissolved. Remove from heat.

Stir in vanilla. Let cool completely, then refrigerate in an airtight container until needed. (Refrigerated sauce will keep for up to 1 week.)

FROZEN TURTLE PIE

Calories 215
Protein 5 g
Carbohydrates 43 g
Fiber 0 g
Total Fat 4 g
  Saturated 0 g
  Polyunsaturated 1 g
  Monounsaturated 2 g
Cholesterol 1 mg
Sodium 126 mg

To assemble, soften ice cream at room temperature for about 15 minutes. Scoop into cooled pie shell and smooth top, mounding slightly. Using your finger, create a well for sauce by making a depression around perimeter, where ice cream meets piecrust. Place in freezer for 30 minutes.

Soften caramel sauce, if necessary, by heating on stovetop over medium-low heat for 2 to 3 minutes or in microwave at 50 percent power (medium) for about 2 minutes. Drizzle sauce over ice cream, allowing sauce to pool around edge. Place in freezer while preparing chocolate sauce.

Melt chocolate chips in top of a double boiler over simmering water (water shouldn't touch bottom of pan), or microwave at 40 percent power for about 5 minutes; drizzle over caramel sauce. Sprinkle pecans over pie. Place in freezer for 30 minutes to 24 hours. To serve, let sit for 5 minutes at room temperature before slicing.

FROZEN TURTLE PIE
WITH CHOCOLATE
CHIPS
Calories 234
Protein 5 g
Carbohydrates 47 g
Fiber 0 g
Total Fat 4g
  Saturated 1 g
  Polyunsaturated 1 g
  Monounsaturated 2 g
Cholesterol 1 mg
Sodium 126 mg

tropical fruit pie

Flavors of summer—this fruit-filled pie is wonderful on a steamy summer evening. For a total change, fill the macaroon crust with lemon sorbet and top it with fresh raspberries—and some candied lemon peel if you want to be fancy.

Vegetable oil spray

macaroon crust

Whites of 4 large eggs, room temperature
2 teaspoons vanilla extract
¼ teaspoon cream of tartar
1¼ cups sugar
½ cup unsweetened flaked coconut

filling

2 cups fresh pineapple chunks
2 cups cantaloupe cubes
1 cup honeydew cubes
1 cup mango cubes
1 medium banana, cut into slices
12 ounces lemon fat-free or low-fat yogurt or 1½ cups frozen fat-free or light whipped topping, thawed

❖

10 to 20 fresh raspberries (optional)
Fresh mint, shredded (optional)

Preheat oven to 325°F. Spray a 10-inch glass pie pan with vegetable oil spray. Set aside.

For crust, in a small mixing bowl, combine egg whites, vanilla, and cream of tartar. With an electric mixer on high, beat until soft peaks form.

Add sugar, 1 to 2 tablespoons at a time, beating after each addition until stiff, glossy peaks form. (Peaks shouldn't fold over when beater is lifted, and meringue shouldn't feel gritty when rubbed between fingers.)

With a rubber scraper, gently fold in coconut. Transfer mixture to pie pan; spread smoothly on bottom and heap on sides and rim.

Bake for 30 to 35 minutes, or until crust is lightly golden, rotating about halfway through. If edges appear to be browning too quickly, cover them lightly with aluminum foil. Turn oven off and let piecrust cool in oven (this prevents cracking).

For filling, in a large bowl, gently combine all ingredients except yogurt.

Using a rubber scraper, fold in yogurt until fruit is well coated. Pour into crust.

Garnish pie with a sprinkling of raspberries and a sprig of fresh mint. Cover and refrigerate until serving time.

Calories 217
Protein 4 g
Carbohydrates 46 g
Fiber 2 g
Total Fat 3 g
  Saturated 2 g
  Polyunsaturated 0 g
  Monounsaturated 0 g
Cholesterol 1 mg
Sodium 52 mg

lighter-than-air lemon pie

When you want to serve a really light dessert, try this delightfully tart treat.
It's best on the day it's baked.

Egg substitute equivalent to 2 eggs
½ cup sugar
3 tablespoons plus 1½ teaspoons
  or 3 tablespoons plus 2 teaspoons
  fresh lemon juice
3 tablespoons water

Whites of 3 large eggs
Pinch of salt
½ cup sugar
1 9-inch low-fat piecrust, such as Basic
  Piecrust (page 74), baked

In top of a double boiler, whisk together egg substitute, ½ cup sugar, lemon juice (add maximum amount if you prefer a tarter pie), and water. Set over boiling water (water shouldn't touch bottom of pan). Cook over high heat until very thick, about 12 minutes, whisking occasionally until mixture is heated through, then whisking constantly. Remove top of double boiler and set aside so mixture can cool slightly.

Preheat oven to 350°F.

In a large mixing bowl, beat egg whites and salt until stiff, using an electric mixer on high.

Beat in remaining sugar, 1 to 2 tablespoons at a time, until very stiff. (Peaks shouldn't fold over when beater is lifted, and meringue shouldn't feel gritty when rubbed between fingers.)

Fold custard into egg white mixture until thoroughly combined. Pour into piecrust, swirling to make peaks on top.

Bake for 7 to 8 minutes, or until peaks brown lightly. Let cool for about 30 minutes before cutting into wedges.

COOK'S TIP ON BEATING EGG WHITES: You can separate eggs much more easily when they're cold, but room-temperature egg whites triple in volume when beaten (not true of cold egg whites). For best results, use a copper, stainless steel, or glass bowl. The bowl and utensils must be extremely clean—any dust or grease may decrease the volume of the egg whites. A plastic bowl will not produce the same volume, and plastic bowls and utensils are more likely to retain the traces of grease that can keep egg whites from beating well.

Calories 192
Protein 5 g
Carbohydrates 39 g
Fiber 0 g
Total Fat 2 g
  Saturated 1 g
  Polyunsaturated 1 g
  Monounsaturated 1 g
Cholesterol 0 mg
Sodium 179 mg

cherry berry pie

This scrumptious and oh-so-simple pie will soon become one of your all-time favorites. Keep your freezer stocked with frozen berries and low-fat piecrusts, and your pantry with pie filling, and you'll be able to pull this dessert together at a moment's notice.

filling

1	21-ounce can cherry pie filling
½	pint fresh or 8 to 10 ounces frozen unsweetened blueberries (1 to 1½ cups)
⅓	cup sugar

½ teaspoon ground cinnamon
¼ teaspoon freshly grated or ground nutmeg

❖

1 9-inch unbaked low-fat piecrust, such as Basic Piecrust (page 74)

Preheat oven to 400°F.

In a large bowl, stir together filling ingredients until thoroughly combined. Spoon into unbaked pie shell.

Bake for 40 to 45 minutes, or until edges of pastry are brown and filling is bubbly. Serve warm or chilled.

COOK'S TIP: You can use the piecrust on page 74, but fit the pastry into a 9-inch pie pan. Flute the edges, then loosely cover the pie pan with plastic wrap or a dish towel while preparing the filling.

COOK'S TIP ON FROZEN BLUEBERRIES: Frozen blueberries don't need to thaw before baking. However, if ice crystals have formed, use cold water to rinse the berries in a colander until the crystals have melted. Drain the berries, then place them on paper towels to remove excess water. Proceed as directed.

Calories 185
Protein 2 g
Carbohydrates 40 g
Fiber 1 g
Total Fat 2 g
  Saturated 1 g
  Polyunsaturated 1 g
  Monounsaturated 1 g
Cholesterol 0 mg
Sodium 115 mg

summertime peach tart

Overlap peach slices to form a rosette for this attractive dessert. It's easy enough for everyday and impressive enough for special occasions.

crust

- 1 cup all-purpose flour
- 2 to 3 tablespoons sugar
- 3 tablespoons light stick margarine, chilled and cut into 1/4-inch cubes
- 1/2 teaspoon vanilla extract
- 2 to 3 tablespoons cold water
  Flour for rolling pastry

filling

- 3 pounds fresh peaches (about 8 medium)
- 1 tablespoon lemon juice
- 2/3 cup sugar
- 2 tablespoons all-purpose flour
- 1 teaspoon ground cinnamon
- 1/4 teaspoon freshly grated or ground nutmeg

Preheat oven to 400°F.

For crust, in a large bowl or food processor, combine flour and sugar.

Add margarine and combine with your fingers or process until mixture resembles coarse meal.

Add vanilla, then add cold water, 1 tablespoon at a time; mix with your fingers or process until dough is manageable (if dough is overworked, it will be tough). Turn dough out onto a lightly floured surface; roll dough into a 12-inch circle. Fold pastry in half and transfer to a 10-inch tart pan with a removable bottom. Unfold pastry and fit into pan. Trim away extra pastry. Prick bottom of shell all over with a fork.

For filling, peel peaches and cut into 1/2-inch slices; put in a large bowl and sprinkle with lemon juice. Set aside.

In a small bowl, combine remaining ingredients. Add to peach mixture, stirring to coat. To form a rosette, begin at outer edge of tart and arrange a row of peach slices facing in one direction. Fill inner section with peach slices facing in opposite direction. Fill in all gaps with remaining peaches.

Measure 1/4 cup liquid remaining in bowl; pour over peaches. Discard remaining liquid. Place tart pan on a baking sheet.

Bake for 40 to 45 minutes, or until edges of pastry are brown and filling is bubbly. Let tart cool for 20 minutes; remove outer ring of pan. Serve tart warm, or chill until ready to serve.

Calories 162
Protein 2 g
Carbohydrates 36 g
Fiber 3 g
Total Fat 2 g
  Saturated 0 g
  Polyunsaturated 1 g
  Monounsaturated 1 g
Cholesterol 0 mg
Sodium 23 mg

mixed berry tart
with apricot glaze

You can enjoy this colorful tart any time of the year. If fresh berries aren't available, substitute kiwifruit, and peaches or nectarines, and canned mandarin orange sections.

crust

1 cup all-purpose flour
2 to 3 tablespoons sugar
3 tablespoons light stick margarine, chilled and cut into 1/4-inch cubes
2 to 3 tablespoons cold water
   Flour for rolling dough

filling

1 3/4 cups fat-free milk
1 small package sugar-free, fat-free (about 1 ounce), or regular (about 3.4 ounces) instant vanilla pudding mix
1 teaspoon vanilla extract or almond extract

topping

1/2 cup fresh raspberries
1/2 cup fresh blueberries
1/2 to 3/4 cup sliced fresh strawberries
1 tablespoon all-fruit apricot spread, lightly beaten with a fork

Preheat oven to 400°F.

For crust, in a large bowl or food processor, combine flour and sugar.

Add margarine and combine with your fingers or process until mixture resembles coarse meal.

Add cold water, 1 tablespoon at a time, and mix with your fingers or process until dough is manageable (if dough is overworked, it will be tough). Turn dough out onto a lightly floured surface; roll dough into a 12-inch circle. Press dough on bottom and up sides of a 9-inch pie pan or a 9-inch tart pan with removable bottom. Prick shell all over with a fork. If desired, cover shell with cooking parchment or aluminum foil and fill with dried beans, uncooked rice, or pie weights.

Bake for 10 minutes. Remove parchment or foil and beans, rice, or pie weights. Bake crust for 15 to 20 minutes, or until golden brown. If edges of crust begin to brown too quickly, cover them with aluminum foil (leave center uncovered). Let cool completely on a cooling rack, about 20 minutes.

For filling, in a medium bowl, combine all ingredients. Whisk for 2 minutes. Pour mixture into cooled crust, cover with plastic wrap, and refrigerate until firm, about 5 minutes.

WITH APRICOT GLAZE

Calories 137
Protein 4 g
Carbohydrates 25 g
Fiber 2 g
Total Fat 2 g
  Saturated 1 g
  Polyunsaturated 1 g
  Monounsaturated 1 g
Cholesterol 1 mg
Sodium 203 mg

Arrange berries on filling, alternating fruits to form decorative concentric circles. Brush top with apricot spread until berries are glazed and shiny (if preserves are thick and unspreadable, warm them slightly in the microwave, 20 to 30 seconds).

VARIATION

Reduce the amount of sugar in the crust to 1 tablespoon. Warm 1 tablespoon all-fruit apricot spread until it melts. As soon as the crust comes out of the oven, brush it with the apricot spread. The crust will absorb the spread and soften.

COOK'S TIP ON BAKING UNFILLED PIECRUSTS: When baking an unfilled crust, or "baking blind," use the weight of dried beans, uncooked rice, or metal or ceramic pie weights to prevent the crust from puffing up and slipping down the sides of the pan. If you don't have any of these, you can nestle a pie pan of equal size into the pan with the uncooked crust, then bake it.

WITH VARIATION
Calories 131
Protein 4 g
Carbohydrates 23 g
Fiber 2 g
Total Fat 2 g
  Saturated 1 g
  Polyunsaturated 1 g
  Monounsaturated 1 g
Cholesterol 1 mg
Sodium 204 mg

fruit platter tart

A winning combination of fresh fruit and orange glaze tops this beautiful dessert. Vary the fruit according to what is in season.

glaze
- 1 cup orange juice
- 2 tablespoons sugar
- 1 tablespoon cornstarch

❖

Vegetable oil spray

crust
- 1 cup all-purpose flour
- 2 tablespoons sugar
- 3 tablespoons light stick margarine, chilled and cut into 1/4-inch cubes

- 2 to 3 tablespoons cold water
- Flour for rolling dough
- 1 tablespoon sugar
- 2 tablespoons red currant jelly

filling
- 2 medium peaches (1/2 to 3/4 pound)
- 1 medium banana
- 1/2 pint fresh raspberries (about 1 cup)
- 1 tablespoon sugar
- 3/4 cup frozen fat-free or light whipped topping, thawed (optional)

For glaze, in a medium saucepan, whisk together all ingredients. Cook over medium heat for 5 minutes, or until thickened, whisking constantly. Remove from heat and let cool for about 30 minutes.

Meanwhile, preheat oven to 400°F. Spray a 12-inch pizza pan with vegetable oil spray.

For crust, in a large bowl or food processor, combine flour and 2 tablespoons sugar.

Add margarine and combine with your fingers or process until mixture resembles coarse meal.

Add cold water, 1 tablespoon at a time, and mix with your fingers or process until dough is manageable (if dough is overworked, it will be tough). Lightly flour a flat surface; roll dough into a 14-inch circle. Fold dough in half and transfer to pizza pan. Make a rim by turning about 1/2 inch of dough toward inside of pan; crimp edges. Prick shell all over with a fork. Sprinkle crust with 1 tablespoon sugar. If desired, cover shell with cooking parchment or aluminum foil and fill with dried beans, uncooked rice, or pie weights. (See Cook's Tip on Baking Unfilled Piecrusts, page 65.)

Bake for 10 minutes. Remove parchment or foil and beans, rice, or pie weights. Bake crust for 5 to 10 minutes, or until golden brown. If edges of crust begin to brown too quickly, cover them with aluminum foil (leave center uncovered). Let cool completely on a cooling rack, about 20 minutes.

Calories 117
Protein 2 g
Carbohydrates 25 g
Fiber 2 g
Total Fat 2 g
  Saturated 0 g
  Polyunsaturated 1 g
  Monounsaturated 0 g
Cholesterol 0 mg
Sodium 21 mg

Meanwhile, in a small saucepan, melt jelly over low heat. Brush over cooled crust.

To assemble, peel peaches; slice about $\frac{1}{2}$ inch thick. Slice banana into pieces about $\frac{1}{2}$ inch thick. Arrange peaches, banana, and raspberries in a decorative pattern on crust. Spoon glaze over fruit. Sprinkle with 1 tablespoon sugar. To serve, cut into 12 wedges. Top each wedge with a dollop of whipped topping.

cinnamon-scented pear crisp

SERVES 8; ABOUT ½ CUP PER SERVING

The tantalizing aroma of cinnamon and brown sugar combined will fill your kitchen as you bake this comforting pear crisp.

filling

- 4 large, firm but ripe pears, such as Anjou or Bartlett (about 2 pounds)
- 1 tablespoon fresh lemon juice
- ¼ cup sugar
- 2 teaspoons cornstarch
- 1 teaspoon ground cinnamon

topping

- ½ cup firmly packed light brown sugar
- ¼ cup quick-cooking oatmeal or rolled oats, uncooked
- ¼ cup all-purpose flour
- 1 teaspoon ground cinnamon
- 3 tablespoons light stick margarine
- 3 tablespoons chopped pecans, dry-roasted

Preheat oven to 375°F.

For filling, peel pears and cut into ¼-inch slices; put into a large bowl and stir in lemon juice.

In a small bowl, stir together remaining filling ingredients. Add to pear mixture, stirring to coat. Let stand for at least 5 minutes.

Meanwhile, for topping, in a medium bowl, combine brown sugar, oatmeal, flour, and cinnamon.

Using a pastry blender, two knives, or a fork, cut in margarine until mixture is crumbly.

Stir in pecans.

Transfer pear mixture to an 11 × 7 × 1½-inch baking dish or 1½-quart baking dish. Sprinkle with topping.

Bake for 30 to 35 minutes, or until topping is golden brown. Let stand for at least 20 minutes. Serve warm or at room temperature.

COOK'S TIP: You can prepare the crisp several hours before serving, then reheat it in a 350°F oven for 10 to 15 minutes, or until warm.

COOK'S TIP ON DRY-ROASTING NUTS: Dry-roasting nuts brings out their flavor. Spread a layer of nuts in an ungreased skillet and dry-roast them over medium heat for 1 to 5 minutes, stirring frequently, or spread them in a shallow baking pan and bake at 350°F for about 5 to 10 minutes, stirring occasionally.

Calories 203
Protein 2 g
Carbohydrates 42 g
Fiber 3 g
Total Fat 5 g
  Saturated 1 g
  Polyunsaturated 1 g
  Monounsaturated 2 g
Cholesterol 0 mg
Sodium 34 mg

home-style
blackberry cobbler

SERVES 8; 3/4 CUP PER SERVING

The "drop on top" crust crowning this cobbler is easier to make than a solid from-scratch piecrust or a lattice piecrust.

Vegetable oil spray

filling

- 2 pounds frozen unsweetened blackberries (about 4 cups) or unsweetened blueberries (4½ to 5 cups), thawed
- ½ cup sugar
- 3 tablespoons reduced-fat biscuit baking mix
- 2 teaspoons lemon juice
- ½ teaspoon vanilla extract

crust

- 1 cup reduced-fat biscuit baking mix
- ⅓ cup fat-free milk
- 2 tablespoons sugar
- ¼ teaspoon grated lemon zest

Preheat oven to 400°F. Spray a 12 × 8 × 2-inch glass baking dish with vegetable oil spray.

For filling, in a large saucepan, stir together all ingredients except vanilla. Bring to a boil over high heat, stirring constantly. Boil for 1 minute, or until slightly thickened. Remove from heat.

Stir vanilla into filling mixture; pour into baking dish.

For crust, in a medium bowl, combine all ingredients, stirring just until blended. Drop batter in eight mounds over filling.

Bake for 25 minutes, or until fruit is bubbly and crust is golden brown around edges. Cobbler will thicken slightly and absorb flavors if allowed to stand for about 20 minutes before serving.

HOME-STYLE PEACH COBBLER

Substitute peaches for blackberries; ½ cup firmly packed dark brown sugar for ½ cup sugar; vanilla, butter, and nut flavoring for vanilla extract; and cinnamon for lemon zest.

HOME-STYLE BLACKBERRY COBBLER

Calories 205
Protein 3 g
Carbohydrates 47 g
Fiber 6 g
Total Fat 2 g
  Saturated 0 g
  Polyunsaturated 0 g
  Monounsaturated 0 g
Cholesterol 0 mg
Sodium 214 mg

HOME-STYLE PEACH COBBLER

Calories 185
Protein 3 g
Carbohydrates 40 g
Fiber 3 g
Total Fat 2 g
  Saturated 0 g
  Polyunsaturated 0 g
  Monounsaturated 0 g
Cholesterol 0 mg
Sodium 218 mg

---

skillet cherry crumble

Keep some canned cherries on hand so you can easily prepare this great pantry dessert without much notice.

topping

2   cups low-fat granola (without raisins)
½   teaspoon ground cinnamon

filling

2   14.5-ounce cans sour pitted cherries in their own juice, undrained
¾   cup sugar
2   tablespoons cornstarch
½   teaspoon vanilla extract or ¼ teaspoon almond extract

For topping, in a small bowl, stir together granola and cinnamon. Set aside.

For filling, in a large nonstick skillet, stir together all ingredients except vanilla until cornstarch has completely dissolved. Bring to a boil over high heat; boil for 2 minutes, or until slightly thickened, stirring constantly. Remove from heat.

Stir in vanilla.

Sprinkle with topping. Let stand for at least 25 minutes to absorb flavors and cool slightly. Serve directly from skillet.

COOK'S TIP: For a crispier topping, add granola mixture after cherries have cooled at least 25 minutes. This dessert is best if eaten within 24 hours. After that, the topping becomes soggy.

Calories 320
Protein 4 g
Carbohydrates 76 g
Fiber 3 g
Total Fat 2 g
  Saturated 0 g
  Polyunsaturated 1 g
  Monounsaturated 0 g
Cholesterol 0 mg
Sodium 90 mg

ricotta pie
with cassis berries

SERVES 8

A perfect after-theater or dinner party dessert, this no-crust pie is delightful whether served warm from the oven or chilled. It's topped with berries marinated in crème de cassis, a liqueur flavored with black currants.

Vegetable oil spray
1 15-ounce container low-fat ricotta cheese
3/4 cup sugar
   Egg substitute equivalent to 1 egg,
   or 1 large egg
1 teaspoon vanilla extract

Whites of 2 large eggs
1 pint fresh blackberries or fresh raspberries
   (about 1 3/4 cups)
3 tablespoons crème de cassis,
   or 3 tablespoons orange juice mixed
   with 1 teaspoon confectioners' sugar

RICOTTA PIE WITH CASSIS BERRIES
Calories 167
Protein 6 g
Carbohydrates 28 g
Fiber 1 g
Total Fat 2 g
Saturated 1 g
Polyunsaturated 0 g
Monounsaturated 1 g
Cholesterol 13 mg
Sodium 74 mg

Preheat oven to 350°F. Spray a 9-inch pie pan with vegetable oil spray.

In a large mixing bowl, whisk together ricotta, sugar, egg substitute, and vanilla until smooth. Set aside.

In a medium mixing bowl, beat egg whites until stiff peaks form. Using a rubber scraper, fold egg whites into ricotta mixture. Pour into pie pan.

Bake for 20 to 25 minutes, or until edges are puffed and slightly brown and center is barely set (doesn't jiggle much when pie is gently shaken; pie will deflate slightly when removed from oven). Let pie cool for 15 minutes on cooling rack.

Meanwhile, in a small bowl, marinate berries for 30 minutes in crème de cassis.

To serve, cut into eight slices and spoon berries over each slice.

RICOTTA PIE WITH CHOCOLATE SYRUP
Substitute 2 tablespoons plus 2 teaspoons fat-free chocolate syrup (1 teaspoon per serving) for the marinated berries.

COOK'S TIP: Low-fat ricotta works better than the fat-free variety in this recipe. The small amount of fat helps hold the filling together and provides smoothness.

RICOTTA PIE WITH CHOCOLATE SYRUP
Calories 152
Protein 6 g
Carbohydrates 26 g
Fiber 0 g
Total Fat 2 g
Saturated 1 g
Polyunsaturated 0 g
Monounsaturated 1 g
Cholesterol 13 mg
Sodium 78 mg

vanilla apples
in phyllo nests

SERVES 8; 1 PHYLLO NEST AND $1/4$ CUP APPLE MIXTURE PER SERVING

Phyllo, which means "leaf" in Greek, is paper-thin sheets of dough. You can use phyllo (FEE-low) in many ways, including as a much-lower-fat replacement for piecrust, as we've done for these delicately sweetened apples. Try this technique of nesting for chiffon mini-pies or simply to hold fresh berries and a bit of whipped topping. Then sit back and enjoy the compliments!

Vegetable oil spray

3 medium Granny Smith apples (about 1 pound)

2 teaspoons lemon juice
Butter-flavor vegetable oil spray

2 sheets frozen phyllo dough, thawed

1 tablespoon acceptable margarine (not light margarine)

$1/4$ cup sugar

2 tablespoons water

$1/2$ teaspoon vanilla extract

1 tablespoon plus 1 teaspoon dried cranberries

$3/4$ teaspoon sugar mixed with scant $1/2$ teaspoon ground cinnamon, or 1 tablespoon plus 1 teaspoon confectioners' sugar

Preheat oven to 350°F. Spray 8 cups of a 12-cup nonstick muffin pan with vegetable oil spray. Set aside.

Peel, core, and cut apples into $1/2$-inch pieces; put in a medium mixing bowl.

Stir lemon juice into apples. Set aside.

Lightly spray both sides of phyllo sheets with butter-flour vegetable oil spray. Stack phyllo sheets. Working quickly so phyllo sheets will not dry out, use a sharp knife to cut each sheet into four lengthwise strips, then cut each strip into fourths crosswise to make thirty-two squares total. Place four squares in each of the prepared muffin cups so they overlap center and edges are overhanging. Press down gently to allow phyllo to take shape of muffin cups. Ruffle overhanging edges to create a nestlike appearance.

Bake for 6 minutes, or until golden. Let cool completely in muffin pan on a cooling rack.

Meanwhile, in a 12-inch nonstick skillet over medium heat, melt margarine. Swirl to coat bottom of skillet.

Sprinkle half the $1/4$ cup sugar in skillet, arrange apples in a single layer on sugar, and top with remaining sugar. Cook for 5 to 6 minutes, or until crisp-tender, *without stirring*. Increase heat to high and, using

Calories 85
Protein 0 g
Carbohydrates 17 g
Fiber 1 g
Total Fat 2 g
    Saturated 0 g
    Polyunsaturated 1 g
    Monounsaturated 1 g
Cholesterol 0 mg
Sodium 40 mg

l o w - f a t   &   l u s c i o u s   d e s s e r t s

two spoons (for more uniform glazing), stir apples for 2 minutes, or until lightly glazed. Remove skillet from heat. Using a slotted spoon, transfer apples to a medium bowl.

Add water to glaze in skillet; cook over high heat for 30 seconds, or until liquid is reduced to 1 tablespoon. Remove from heat.

Add vanilla, stirring well, then stir into apples. Let cool completely, about 20 minutes.

To serve, place phyllo nests on individual dessert plates, spoon about ¼ cup apples into each nest, and sprinkle each with cranberries and cinnamon sugar. Serve immediately.

COOK'S TIP: You can prepare the phyllo nests and the apples up to 24 hours in advance and assemble the dessert at serving time. Cover the apples with plastic wrap and refrigerate. Remove them from the refrigerator about 30 minutes before serving. Leave the phyllo nests in the muffin tins, wrap them completely in plastic wrap, and store them in a cool, dry area, such as on the counter or in the pantry.

basic piecrust

If you've been looking for a low-fat piecrust that tastes good and has a pleasant texture, your search is over. This crust is perfect for everything from savory dishes such as spinach quiche to sweet treats such as chocolate meringue pie—made with heart-healthful ingredients, of course.

1 cup all-purpose flour	4 to 6 tablespoons ice water
¼ teaspoon salt	1 teaspoon vinegar
4 tablespoons light stick margarine, cut into 4 pieces	Vegetable oil spray

In a medium bowl, stir together flour and salt.

Using a pastry blender, a fork, or two knives, cut margarine into flour until mixture looks crumbly.

Add 4 tablespoons water and vinegar; using a fork, gently fold mixture until liquid is incorporated and dough starts to hold together when pressed lightly with fingers; don't try to shape it into a ball. If it doesn't hold together, gradually add remaining water as needed to reach this stage.

Place dough in center of a large sheet of plastic wrap, plastic wrap over dough to seal; gently pressing dough together, shape it into a disk about 5 inches in diameter. Refrigerate for 30 minutes to 24 hours. Break off a small piece from one end. If it crumbles, dough is too dry; sprinkle with 1 to 2 teaspoons water and reshape. Refrigerate for 5 minutes. (At this stage, you can put dough in an airtight freezer bag or other airtight container and freeze it for up to one month. Let it thaw for about 30 minutes at room temperature or for up to 8 hours in the refrigerator before using.)

Preheat oven to 425°F for baking unfilled crust. Spray a 9-inch pie pan with vegetable oil spray.

Place dough on a sheet of wax paper; generously sprinkle both sides of dough with flour; shake off any excess flour. Top with another sheet of wax paper. Roll out dough to ⅛-inch thickness (about 11 inches in diameter). Remove top sheet of wax paper, invert dough into pie pan, and remove remaining sheet of wax paper. Be careful not to stretch dough or it will shrink when it bakes. Trim edges and flute with a fork or your fingers. For baking an unfilled crust, prick shell all over with a fork. If desired, cover shell with cooking parchment or aluminum foil and fill with dried beans, uncooked rice, or pie weights. (See Cook's Tip on Baking Unfilled Piecrusts, page 65.)

Calories 82
Protein 2 g
Carbohydrates 12 g
Fiber 0 g
Total Fat 3 g
　Saturated 1 g
　Polyunsaturated 1 g
　Monounsaturated 1 g
Cholesterol 0 mg
Sodium 111 mg

If your recipe calls for a partially baked unfilled crust, bake for 10 minutes, or until surface is dry. To fully bake an unfilled crust, bake for 13 to 15 minutes, or until edges are golden brown. To bake an uncooked crust and filling together, use directions in recipe for filling.

COOK'S TIP: Add a couple of pinches of ground cinnamon, nutmeg, or ginger to the flour and salt to flavor your piecrust.

COOK'S TIP ON PIECRUST: It's easy to roll your piecrust to the proper size if you use wax paper and a dark, thin marker. Sprinkle a few drops of water on the countertop to hold the wax paper in place. Draw the outline of the rim of the pie pan on the wax paper, then flip the wax paper over (drawn line will show through). Place a second sheet of wax paper over the dough, then roll the dough until it's the same size as the circle.

cakes

Super Chocolaty Cake

German Chocolate Cake with
Pecan Coconut Frosting

Double-Chocolate
Valentine Cake

Deep, Dark Chocolate
Pudding Cake

Mochaccino Pudding Cake

pies

Fudgy Chocolate
Walnut Pie

Mocha Fudge Angel Pie

Frozen Chocolate
Peppermint Patty Pie

pudding and soufflés

Chocolate Orange
Bread Pudding

Chocolate
Mini-Soufflés

Frozen Chocolate
Mini-Soufflés

cookies

Chunky Chocolate
Chip Cookies

Chocolate Chip Cookies

Mocha Chip Cookies

Chocolate-Orange Cookies

Holiday Chippers

Cocoa Mint Kisses

Speckled Mint Kisses

Cocoa Mint Vacherins

Chocolate Peanut Butter
Swirl Cookies

Chocolate Walnut Brownies

sauce and icings

Chocolate Rum Sauce

Fudge Icing

Creamy Milk
Chocolate Icing

chocolate, chocolate, chocolate

super chocolaty cake

Nestle fresh strawberries, raspberries, and kiwifruit slices in the icing just before serving for a beautiful presentation. If you prefer a chocolate icing, try Whipped Cocoa Icing, below; Fudge Icing (page 100); or Creamy Milk Chocolate Icing (page 101).

Vegetable oil spray (optional)

cake

- 1¾ cups all-purpose flour
- 1¾ cups firmly packed light brown sugar
- ¾ cup unsweetened cocoa powder (Dutch process preferred)
- 1½ teaspoons baking soda
- 1½ teaspoons baking powder
- 1¼ cups fat-free or low-fat buttermilk
- ¼ cup fat-free tub margarine, melted
  Whites of 2 large eggs

- 1 large egg, or egg substitute equivalent to 1 egg
- 1½ teaspoons vanilla extract
- 1 cup boiling water

icing

- ½ cup fat-free milk, chilled
- 1 1.3-ounce package powdered whipped topping mix
- 1 teaspoon vanilla extract
- 1 tablespoon unsweetened cocoa powder (optional)

Preheat oven to 350°F. Spray two 9-inch round or square cake pans with vegetable oil spray or line with cooking parchment. Set aside.

For cake, in a large bowl, combine flour, brown sugar, cocoa powder, baking soda, and baking powder. Combine well with a fork to break up sugar.

In a large mixing bowl, combine remaining cake ingredients except water. Beat with an electric mixer on low just until blended.

Gradually beat in boiling water.

Gradually add flour mixture while beating on low just until blended; don't overbeat. Divide batter evenly between two pans.

Bake for 30 minutes, or until a toothpick inserted in center comes out clean. Let cake cool in pans on cooling racks for 10 minutes. Invert cakes onto racks, remove pans, and let cakes cool completely.

Meanwhile, for icing, combine all ingredients in a large mixing bowl. Beat with an electric mixer on low until blended. Increase setting to high and beat until stiff peaks form, about 4 minutes; fold in cocoa powder. Cover and refrigerate until ready to use.

To assemble cake, place one layer on a serving plate. Spread 1 cup icing over top. Repeat with second cake layer and remaining icing. Using back of a spoon, make swirling motions to form a decorative design.

Calories 255
Protein 6 g
Carbohydrates 53 g
Fiber 2 g
Total Fat 2 g
  Saturated 1 g
  Polyunsaturated 0 g
  Monounsaturated 0 g
Cholesterol 19 mg
Sodium 311 mg

COOK'S TIP: Ordinarily, we suggest gathering all the ingredients for a recipe before you begin preparing it. Here, however, it's best to keep the milk in the refrigerator until you're ready to beat the icing. The chilled milk will yield a higher volume than milk at room temperature.

COOK'S TIP ON WHIPPED TOPPING MIX: Look for envelopes of powdered whipped topping mix near pudding and gelatin mixes at the grocery store. In addition to being used for frosting, the mix can be used to lighten the texture of cream pies and make them even creamier.

german chocolate cake with pecan coconut frosting

SERVES 12

With its rich-tasting topping, this delectable cake is still moist days after you bake it.

Vegetable oil spray

cake

2	cups all-purpose flour
¾	cup unsweetened cocoa powder (Dutch process preferred)
1	teaspoon baking soda
2	cups sugar
8	ounces fat-free tub margarine (1 small tub)
	Egg substitute equivalent to 2 eggs, or 2 large eggs
1	teaspoon vanilla extract
1	cup fat-free or low-fat buttermilk
	Whites of 4 large eggs

frosting

1	cup plus 2 tablespoons fat-free evaporated milk
¾	cup firmly packed light brown sugar
¼	cup fat-free tub margarine
3	tablespoons egg substitute or white of 1 large egg
⅓	cup unsweetened flaked coconut, toasted
⅓	cup pecans, chopped and dry-roasted (see Cook's Tip on Dry-Roasting Nuts, page 68)
1½	teaspoons vanilla extract

Preheat oven to 350°F. Spray two 9-inch round cake pans with vegetable oil spray. Set aside.

For cake, in a medium bowl, blend flour, cocoa powder, and baking soda. Set aside.

In a large mixing bowl, beat sugar and margarine together with an electric mixer until light and fluffy.

Slowly beat in egg substitute.

Beat vanilla into sugar mixture (batter may look curdled).

Gradually add flour mixture alternately with buttermilk, beating on low after each addition.

In a large mixing bowl, with an electric mixer on medium, beat egg whites until firm but not stiff peaks form; fold into batter just until combined. Divide evenly between two cake pans.

Bake for 30 to 40 minutes, or until a toothpick inserted in center comes out clean and cake springs back when lightly pressed in center. Let cool in pans on cooling racks for 10 minutes. Invert cakes onto racks, remove pans, and let cakes cool for 1 hour before frosting.

Calories 364
Protein 9 g
Carbohydrates 71 g
Fiber 3 g
Total Fat 5 g
  Saturated 2 g
  Polyunsaturated 1 g
  Monounsaturated 2 g
Cholesterol 2 mg
Sodium 362 mg

low-fat & luscious desserts

Meanwhile, for frosting, in a medium, heavy saucepan, whisk together milk, brown sugar, margarine, and egg substitute. Bring to a low boil over medium heat; cook for 8 minutes, or until mixture thickens, whisking constantly.

Stir in remaining ingredients; let cool to room temperature.

To assemble, place one cake layer on serving plate; spread half of frosting on top only. Set second cake layer on frosting; spread remaining frosting on top only.

COOK'S TIP: To cool icing quickly, spread it in a thin layer on a baking sheet.

double-chocolate valentine cake

SERVES 12

*You don't have to wait until Valentine's Day to enjoy this heart-shaped delight.
It's also lovely for birthdays and other festive occasions.*

Vegetable oil spray

cake

1	cup all-purpose flour
1/2	cup unsweetened cocoa powder (Dutch process preferred)
3/4	teaspoon baking soda
1/2	teaspoon salt
1/4	teaspoon baking powder
1/2	cup sugar
1/2	cup firmly packed golden or light brown sugar
1/2	cup fat-free milk
2	tablespoons acceptable vegetable oil
2	tablespoons unsweetened applesauce
1	teaspoon vanilla extract
	Whites of 2 large eggs
1/4	teaspoon cream of tartar

chocolate glaze

2 1/2	cups sifted confectioners' sugar
2	to 4 tablespoons coffee
1/4	cup unsweetened cocoa powder (Dutch process preferred)
1/4	cup fat-free milk
1/4	teaspoon vanilla extract

white glaze

2/3	cup sifted confectioners' sugar
1	tablespoon fat-free milk

Preheat oven to 350°F. Spray an 8- or 9-inch heart-shaped or round baking pan with vegetable oil spray. Set aside.

For cake, in a medium bowl, stir together flour, cocoa powder, baking soda, salt, and baking powder.

In a large bowl, whisk together sugars, 1/2 cup milk, oil, and applesauce until smooth.

Gradually whisk flour mixture into sugar mixture, blending well.

Stir in vanilla.

In a medium bowl, with an electric mixer on high, beat egg whites and cream of tartar until stiff. (Peaks shouldn't fold over when beater is lifted.) Using a rubber scraper, gently fold egg whites into batter until completely incorporated (no whites should be visible). Pour batter into pan.

Bake for 30 to 35 minutes, or until a toothpick inserted in center comes out clean.

Calories 256
Protein 3 g
Carbohydrates 55 g
Fiber 2 g
Total Fat 3 g
  Saturated 1 g
  Polyunsaturated 1 g
  Monounsaturated 1 g
Cholesterol 0 mg
Sodium 210 mg

low-fat & luscious desserts

Set cooling rack on a large piece of wax paper (to catch drips from glaze). Let cake cool in pan on cooling rack for 20 minutes. Invert cake onto rack, remove pan, and allow cake to finish cooling.

For chocolate glaze, in a medium bowl, whisk together ingredients. When cake is completely cool, spread glaze over cake, allowing glaze to run down sides.

For white glaze, in a small bowl, whisk together ingredients. Snip one corner from a small plastic bag to form a tiny hole; pour glaze into bag. Squeeze glaze in thin, parallel lines about $\frac{1}{2}$ to 1 inch apart horizontally across top of cake. At $\frac{1}{2}$- to 1-inch intervals, pull vertically over top of cake with a sharp knife, bamboo skewer, or toothpick, drawing through lines of white glaze and across the chocolate, creating a feathered pattern. When glaze has dried, transfer cake to serving platter.

> COOK'S TIP: After spreading the chocolate glaze over the cake, you can use a thin, sharp object, such as a knife, to lightly mark where to draw the lines of white glaze. If you make a big mistake, smooth that part of the glaze and try again. Don't worry if the lines aren't perfectly straight.

deep, dark chocolate pudding cake

SERVES 8; ABOUT $^3/_4$ CUP PER SERVING

This cake is so chocolaty and fudgy! As it bakes, a cake layer forms on top and a rich, thick pudding layer settles to the bottom.

Vegetable oil spray
1 cup cake flour
$^2/_3$ cup sugar
$^1/_4$ cup unsweetened cocoa powder (Dutch process preferred)
2 teaspoons baking powder
Pinch of salt

$^1/_2$ cup fat-free milk
1 tablespoon acceptable vegetable oil
$^1/_2$ teaspoon vanilla extract
$^2/_3$ cup sugar
$^1/_4$ cup unsweetened cocoa powder (Dutch process preferred)
1 cup boiling water

Preheat oven to 350°F. Spray a 2-quart (8-inch) soufflé dish with vegetable oil spray.

In a large bowl, whisk together flour, $^2/_3$ cup sugar, $^1/_4$ cup cocoa powder, baking powder, and salt.

Whisk in milk, oil, and vanilla. Scrape batter into soufflé dish, smoothing top with a metal spatula or rubber scraper (batter will be very thick).

In a small bowl, combine remaining $^2/_3$ cup sugar and $^1/_4$ cup cocoa powder. Sprinkle evenly over batter.

Carefully pour boiling water over all. Do not stir.

Bake for 25 to 30 minutes, or until top of cake looks dry and a toothpick inserted into *top* cake layer comes out clean. (A crust will have formed and pudding underneath may bubble around edges.) Let cool on a cooling rack for 5 minutes. Serve immediately.

MOCHACCINO PUDDING CAKE
Add $^1/_2$ teaspoon cinnamon to flour mixture, and replace boiling water with boiling extra-strong coffee.

Calories 234
Protein 3 g
Carbohydrates 51 g
Fiber 2 g
Total Fat 2 g
  Saturated 1 g
  Polyunsaturated 1 g
  Monounsaturated 1 g
Cholesterol 0 mg
Sodium 152 mg

low-fat & luscious desserts

chunky chocolate chip cookies

SERVES 27; 2 COOKIES PER SERVING

Rich and soft, these cookies will satisfy your chocolate craving—three ways!

Vegetable oil spray (optional)
1 cup unsweetened baby food prunes with applesauce or 1 cup pureed dried prunes
3/4 cup sugar
3/4 cup firmly packed light brown sugar
Whites of 3 large eggs
1 teaspoon vanilla extract

2 cups all-purpose flour
1/4 cup unsweetened cocoa powder
1 teaspoon baking soda
1/2 teaspoon salt
1 cup reduced-fat semisweet chocolate chips
4 ounces bittersweet chocolate, cut into pea-size pieces

Preheat oven to 375°F. Line two baking sheets with cooking parchment, or spray baking sheets with vegetable oil spray. Set aside.

In a large mixing bowl, stir or beat prunes and sugars together until soft and creamy.

Using a rubber scraper, fold in egg whites and vanilla.

In a medium bowl, stir together flour, cocoa powder, baking soda, and salt. Stir into prune mixture, blending well.

Stir in chocolate chips and chunks. Drop by heaping teaspoonfuls onto baking sheets. Moisten palm of your hand with water; slightly flatten each cookie to about 2 inches in diameter.

Bake for 10 minutes, or until firm. Transfer cookies, still on cooking parchment, to cooling racks. To prevent sticking, remove cookies from cooking parchment as soon as they cool.

COOK'S TIP ON COOKING PARCHMENT: To help keep baked goods from burning on the bottom, line baking sheets and pans with cooking parchment. Cooking parchment also helps make cleanup a breeze when you're baking cookies—no more scouring your baking sheets. If the cooking parchment tends to roll up when you use it to line baking sheets, start by dropping the dough for one cookie at each corner. Look in supermarkets and specialty stores for cooking parchment in rolls, as well as in packages of pieces precut to fit 8- and 9-inch cake pans.

To save cleanup time, replace the cooking parchment for additional batches of cookies instead of washing the baking sheets.

Calories 148
Protein 2 g
Carbohydrates 30 g
Fiber 1 g
Total Fat 3 g
  Saturated 2 g
  Polyunsaturated 0 g
  Monounsaturated 0 g
Cholesterol 0 mg
Sodium 99 mg

chocolate chip cookies

SERVES 15; 1 COOKIE PER SERVING

Full of chocolate chips and brown sugar, these cookies will hit the spot when you want old-fashioned goodness.

Vegetable oil spray (optional)
¼ cup light stick margarine, softened
⅔ cup firmly packed light brown sugar
Egg substitute equivalent to 1 egg, or 1 large egg

½ teaspoon vanilla extract
1 cup all-purpose flour
½ teaspoon baking soda
Pinch of salt
½ cup reduced-fat semisweet chocolate chips

Preheat oven to 350°F. Line two baking sheets with cooking parchment, or spray with vegetable oil spray. Set aside.

In a large mixing bowl, using an electric mixer on medium, cream margarine until smooth, about 2 minutes.

Increase setting to medium-high and gradually add brown sugar, beating for 3 minutes.

Add egg substitute and vanilla; beat until blended, scraping bowl once or twice (mixture will be very thin).

In a small bowl, combine flour, baking soda, and salt. Add to margarine mixture in two or three batches, beating or stirring in with a wooden spoon just until blended.

Stir in chocolate chips.

Scoop six mounds of dough, each about ⅛ cup (2 tablespoons), onto each baking sheet (some dough will remain); leave 2 inches between cookies.

Bake for 8 to 10 minutes, rotating sheets front to back after 4 to 5 minutes. Cookies will be slightly darker around edges, puffed and lighter in middle. Leave cookies on sheets and let cool on cooling racks. When baking sheets are cooled completely, about 10 minutes, repeat with remaining dough for final three cookies. (Cooking parchment will probably be reusable.) Cookies are best within one day of baking but can be stored in an airtight container at room temperature for up to four days.

CHOCOLATE CHIP COOKIES	3
Calories 115	
Protein 2 g	
Carbohydrates 22 g	
Fiber 0 g	
Total Fat 3 g	
Saturated 1 g	
Polyunsaturated 0 g	
Monounsaturated 0 g	
Cholesterol 0 mg	
Sodium 84 mg	

MOCHA CHIP COOKIES

Dissolve 1 teaspoon instant coffee granules in 1 teaspoon hot water. Add with egg substitute and vanilla.

CHOCOLATE-ORANGE COOKIES

Add 2 teaspoons grated orange zest and 1 teaspoon orange-flavored liqueur (optional) with egg substitute and vanilla.

HOLIDAY CHIPPERS

Add ¼ cup dried cranberries with chocolate chips.

cocoa mint kisses

SERVES 18; 2 KISSES PER SERVING

These small cookies are as light as air but pack a lot of mint chocolate flavor.

Vegetable oil spray (optional)
Whites of 3 large eggs, room temperature
1/4 teaspoon cream of tartar
3/4 cup sugar

1/2 teaspoon vanilla extract
1/2 teaspoon peppermint extract
2 tablespoons sifted unsweetened cocoa powder (Dutch process preferred)

Preheat oven to 250°F. Line two baking sheets with cooking parchment, or lightly spray with vegetable oil spray.

In a large mixing bowl, beat egg whites with an electric mixer on medium until frothy.

Add cream of tartar and beat until soft peaks form, 2 to 4 minutes.

Add sugar, 1 to 2 tablespoons at a time, beating on high after each addition until stiff, glossy peaks form. (Peaks shouldn't fold over when beater is lifted, and meringue shouldn't feel grainy when rubbed with fingers.)

Quickly beat in extracts.

With a rubber scraper, fold in cocoa powder until batter is uniform in color.

Using two teaspoons, drop walnut-size mounds of meringue onto baking sheets, leaving 1 inch between cookies. For a spiky look, use a fork to create a peak on top of each cookie. Or spoon meringue into a pastry bag fitted with a 1/2-inch open star tip and pipe into 1-inch rosettes.

Bake for 40 to 45 minutes, or until kisses are dry to the touch. Transfer cookies, still on cooking parchment, to cooling racks; let cool completely, about 20 minutes, then peel from paper and store in an airtight container for up to 10 days. (Don't store with any other cookies or they'll taste of mint too.)

COCOA MINT KISSES

Calories 38
Protein 1 g
Carbohydrates 9 g
Fiber 0 g
Total Fat 0 g
 Saturated 0 g
 Polyunsaturated 0 g
 Monounsaturated 0 g
Cholesterol 0 mg
Sodium 10 mg

SPECKLED MINT KISSES

Substitute 1 ounce coarsely grated unsweetened chocolate for cocoa powder. Don't use a pastry bag; chocolate flecks will clog the decorator's tip.

COCOA MINT VACHERINS

For a meringue nest, or vacherin, drop about $\frac{1}{4}$ cup batter onto a baking sheet lined with cooking parchment. Using the back of a tablespoon, make a smooth indentation about the size of a walnut in the center. Repeat with remaining batter, making eight more mounds about 2 inches apart. Bake at 250°F for about 1 hour, or until dry to the touch. Use as an edible serving dish for pudding, fruit, sorbet, or fat-free ice cream or frozen yogurt. Serves 9; 1 vacherin per serving.

COOK'S TIP: A handy way to get the meringue onto the baking sheets is to use two teaspoons, one to measure the batter and one to slide it out of the first spoon.

COOK'S TIP ON COCOA POWDER: If your cocoa powder has lumps in it, sift it so your measurements will be accurate and so the powder will be easy to incorporate.

SPECKLED MINT KISSES	
Calories 44	
Protein 1 g	
Carbohydrates 9 g	
Fiber 0 g	
Total Fat 1 g	
Saturated 1 g	
Polyunsaturated 0 g	
Monounsaturated 0 g	
Cholesterol 0 mg	
Sodium 10 mg	

COCOA MINT VACHERINS	
Calories 76	
Protein 2 g	
Carbohydrates 18 g	
Fiber 0 g	
Total Fat 0 g	
Saturated 0 g	
Polyunsaturated 0 g	
Monounsaturated 0 g	
Cholesterol 0 mg	
Sodium 19 mg	

Sauces
Syrups

chocolate peanut butter swirl cookies

Swirl together two favorites, peanut butter and chocolate, for a yummy, eye-catching cookie.

peanut butter dough

1¼ cups all-purpose flour
1 teaspoon baking powder
½ cup sugar
¼ cup reduced-fat creamy peanut butter
2 tablespoons light stick margarine, softened
2 tablespoons egg substitute
2 tablespoons fat-free milk

chocolate dough

1 cup all-purpose flour
3 tablespoons unsweetened cocoa powder (Dutch process preferred)
1 teaspoon baking powder
½ cup sugar
2 tablespoons acceptable margarine, softened
2 tablespoons egg substitute
2 tablespoons light corn syrup
1 tablespoon fat-free milk

❖

Vegetable oil spray

For peanut butter dough, in a small bowl, combine flour and baking powder.

In a large mixing bowl, beat sugar, peanut butter, and margarine with an electric mixer on medium.

Beat in egg substitute and milk.

Gradually add flour mixture to peanut butter mixture, beating after each addition. Put dough on plastic wrap and shape into a rectangle about 5 × 7 inches; wrap dough and refrigerate for 1 hour to two days.

For chocolate dough, in a small bowl, stir together flour, cocoa powder, and baking powder.

In a large bowl, stir together sugar and margarine.

Add egg substitute, corn syrup, and milk to sugar mixture; beat until thoroughly combined.

Gradually add flour mixture to sugar mixture, beating after each addition. Shape, wrap, and chill as directed above for peanut butter dough.

Preheat oven to 350°F. Spray two baking sheets with vegetable oil spray. Set aside.

Calories 111
Protein 2 g
Carbohydrates 20 g
Fiber 1 g
Total Fat 3 g
  Saturated 1 g
  Polyunsaturated 1 g
  Monounsaturated 1 g
Cholesterol 0 mg
Sodium 82 mg

Tear off four pieces of plastic wrap, each about 18 inches long. Put one piece on a large cutting board. Put peanut butter dough on plastic wrap. Put another piece of plastic wrap on dough. Roll dough to ¼-inch thickness, retaining rectangular shape. Set aside. Repeat procedure with chocolate dough.

Remove top piece of plastic wrap from both doughs. Place unwrapped side of chocolate dough on unwrapped side of peanut butter dough. Carefully peel plastic wrap from top side of chocolate dough. Using both hands, lift one long end of plastic wrap, folding dough over, jelly-roll style, to form a cylinder. Put dough on cutting board; cut crosswise into ¼-inch slices and place on baking sheets.

Bake for 12 minutes, or until cookies are slightly golden on bottom. Remove cookies from baking sheets and let cool on cooling racks.

COOK'S TIP ON DUTCH PROCESS UNSWEETENED COCOA POWDER: Many recipes in this cookbook call for Dutch process unsweetened cocoa powder, sometimes referred to as dark, European-style cocoa powder. Look for it in the baking section of the grocery. Dutch process unsweetened cocoa powder goes through a special process that helps neutralize acidity. You can replace regular unsweetened cocoa powder with the Dutch process variety when you want a deeper color and a more intense flavor.

COOK'S TIP FOR CUTTING COOKIES: An easy way to cut cylinders of refrigerated cookie dough is to use dental floss (waxed or unwaxed) in a sawing motion instead of using a knife.

chocolate walnut brownies

SERVES 16; 1 BROWNIE PER SERVING

When you crave a chewy chocolate dessert, nothing beats a good brownie. This standout version boasts a topping of nuts and toasted wheat germ. Enjoy one with an ice-cold glass of fat-free milk.

Vegetable oil spray
¾ cup all-purpose flour
2 tablespoons plus 1½ teaspoons unsweetened cocoa powder (Dutch process preferred)
1 teaspoon baking powder
1 cup sugar
2 tablespoons acceptable margarine, softened

Egg substitute equivalent to 1 egg, or 1 large egg
2 tablespoons unsweetened applesauce
1 teaspoon vanilla extract
2 tablespoons chopped walnuts
2 tablespoons toasted wheat germ

Preheat oven to 350°F. Spray an 8-inch square baking pan with vegetable oil spray. Set aside.

In a medium bowl, combine flour, cocoa powder, and baking powder.

In another medium bowl, cream sugar and margarine with an electric mixer on medium for 1 minute.

Add egg substitute, applesauce, and vanilla, beating until combined.

Stir in flour mixture; beat on low just until combined. Pour batter into baking pan, then sprinkle with walnuts and wheat germ.

Bake for 20 to 23 minutes, or until a toothpick inserted in center comes out clean. Let cool slightly on a cooling rack before cutting into 16 bars.

COOK'S TIP ON TOASTED WHEAT GERM: At the heart of a wheat kernel lies a nutrition-packed morsel known as wheat germ. Available toasted or untoasted, it should be refrigerated (for up to six months) or frozen (up to one year) so it won't go rancid. Look for new flavors, such as honey crunch, which is delicious in this recipe. Sprinkle small amounts of wheat germ over your favorite frozen-yogurt sundae, low-fat pudding, or cake, or stir 1 tablespoon into a glass of your favorite fruit smoothie for a nutrition boost.

Calories 99
Protein 2 g
Carbohydrates 18 g
Fiber 1 g
Total Fat 2 g
  Saturated 0 g
  Polyunsaturated 1 g
  Monounsaturated 1 g
Cholesterol 0 mg
Sodium 54 mg

fudgy chocolate walnut pie

SERVES 8

All you need for chocolate bliss is a pie pan, a saucepan, a little stirring—and this fabulous recipe.

Vegetable oil spray
1/2 cup reduced-fat thin chocolate wafer cookie crumbs or chocolate graham cracker crumbs (about 10 wafers or 8 graham cracker squares)
1 cup sugar
3/4 cup fat-free evaporated milk

1/2 cup light corn syrup
3 tablespoons unsweetened cocoa powder (Dutch process preferred)
3 tablespoons semisweet chocolate chips
Egg substitute equivalent to 3 eggs
2 tablespoons chopped walnuts

Preheat oven to 350°F.

Spray a 9-inch pie pan with vegetable oil spray. Using your hands, pat crumbs on bottom of pie pan.

In a medium saucepan, whisk together sugar, milk, and corn syrup; cook over medium heat until sugar has dissolved, 3 to 4 minutes, whisking occasionally. Remove from heat.

Whisk in cocoa powder and chocolate chips. Let mixture stand for 5 minutes, whisking occasionally to help it cool slightly.

Whisk egg substitute into chocolate mixture until smooth; pour into pie pan. Sprinkle with walnuts. Place pie pan on a baking sheet.

Bake for 35 to 40 minutes, or until center is set (doesn't jiggle when pie is gently shaken). Let pie cool on cooling rack for 30 minutes. Serve warm or chilled.

COOK'S TIP ON THIN CHOCOLATE WAFER COOKIES: Use these dark, slender cookies as creative garnishes. Here are just a few ideas: Insert a whole wafer on top of a scoop of nonfat frozen yogurt, break wafers into irregular pieces and arrange them on a low-fat custard pie, or sprinkle crumbs over pudding made with fat-free milk.

Calories 240
Protein 5 g
Carbohydrates 51 g
Fiber 1 g
Total Fat 3 g
  Saturated 1 g
  Polyunsaturated 1 g
  Monounsaturated 1 g
Cholesterol 1 mg
Sodium 111 mg

mocha fudge angel pie

SERVES 8

Showy enough for company, this chocoholics' delight has less than 2 grams of saturated fat per serving.

Vegetable oil spray
Flour for dusting pie pan

meringue shell

Whites of 3 large eggs, room temperature
¼ teaspoon cream of tartar
¼ teaspoon vanilla extract
¾ cup sugar

filling

1 14-ounce can fat-free sweetened condensed milk
¼ cup unsweetened cocoa powder (Dutch process preferred)
1 square unsweetened chocolate
1½ teaspoons unflavored gelatin
¼ cup water
1 tablespoon to 1 tablespoon plus 1½ teaspoons instant coffee granules (chocolate roast or regular)
8 ounces frozen fat-free or light whipped topping, thawed (about 3 cups)

Preheat oven to 275°F. Spray a 9-inch pie pan with vegetable oil spray and dust with flour; shake out excess flour.

For meringue shell, in a large mixing bowl, beat egg whites with an electric mixer on high until foamy.

Sprinkle cream of tartar and vanilla over egg whites and continue beating until soft peaks form.

Gradually add sugar, 1 to 2 tablespoons at a time, beating after each addition until stiff, glossy peaks form. (Peaks shouldn't fold over when beater is lifted, and meringue shouldn't feel gritty when rubbed between fingers.) Spread meringue in pie pan, shaping it into a shell with sides about 2 inches high.

Bake for 1 hour. Turn oven off and let shell cool in oven for 2 hours.

Meanwhile, for filling, combine milk, cocoa powder, and chocolate in a medium microwave-safe bowl or small, heavy saucepan. Microwave on 100 percent power (high) for 2 to 4 minutes, stirring once or twice, or cook over low heat, stirring constantly, until chocolate has melted and mixture is smooth.

In a small bowl, combine gelatin, water, and coffee granules. Let stand until gelatin is softened, about 5 minutes. Stir into hot chocolate mixture. Let cool to room temperature, about 30 minutes. With an electric mixer, beat on high for 5 minutes, or until mixture is light.

Calories 300
Protein 7 g
Carbohydrates 62 g
Fiber 1 g
Total Fat 2 g
  Saturated 1 g
  Polyunsaturated 0 g
  Monounsaturated 1 g
Cholesterol 3 mg
Sodium 91 mg

Fold in whipped topping; spoon into baked shell. Cover with plastic wrap and refrigerate until set, 2 to 3 hours. If you prefer, store unfilled baked shell at room temperature in an airtight container for up to two days or freeze for several weeks. Fill, then refrigerate until set. (Frozen shell doesn't need to thaw first.)

COOK'S TIP: If you freeze this pie, serve it while it's still a little frozen for the best texture. Freeze the pie uncovered, then place it in a jumbo airtight freezer bag or cover it with plastic wrap. It will store well for up to one month.

COOK'S TIP ON MERINGUE SHELLS: Try to bake meringue shells when the weather isn't humid. They'll be less likely to bead and become gooey.

frozen chocolate peppermint patty pie

For a fun family project, make this dessert with your children. They'll enjoy "helping" you.

15 thin chocolate wafer cookies
3 large or 9 small chocolate-covered
   peppermint patties (4½ ounces), broken
   into bite-size pieces
1 tablespoon water

1 quart chocolate nonfat frozen yogurt or
   fat-free ice cream
8 ounces frozen fat-free or light whipped
   topping, thawed (about 3 cups)

In a food processor, process cookies into fine crumbs. With machine running, gradually add patties, processing until well blended. Continue processing, adding water to create a coarse crumble texture.

To assemble, put frozen yogurt into an 8-inch square baking pan. Using back of a spoon or a fork, spread to smooth. Cover with whipped topping; crumble cookie mixture evenly over all. Cover tightly with plastic wrap and place in freezer for 8 hours or overnight. Let pie sit on counter for about 20 minutes to soften slightly before serving. Pie can be frozen for up to one week.

COOK'S TIP ON WRAPPING FROZEN PIES: To protect frozen pies from any contact with air that can cause off flavors and ice crystals, wrap pies well with plastic wrap. Tightly wrap a continuous sheet of plastic wrap completely over top, side, bottom, and other side of pie; turn pie and wrap another continuous sheet of plastic wrap in the opposite direction. Tape the edges.

Calories 239
Protein 4 g
Carbohydrates 48 g
Fiber 1 g
Total Fat 3 g
  Saturated 1 g
  Polyunsaturated 1 g
  Monounsaturated 1 g
Cholesterol 1 mg
Sodium 125 mg

low-fat & luscious desserts

chocolate orange bread pudding

*Enjoy the flavorful combination of orange and chocolate in this moist bread pudding.
It's divine plain, or to gild the lily, serve it with Chocolate Rum Sauce (page 99).*

Vegetable oil spray
1 pound French bread, torn into bite-size pieces
3 cups fat-free milk
1¾ cups sugar
¾ cup unsweetened cocoa powder
Egg substitute equivalent to 1 egg, or 1 large egg

2 tablespoons orange zest (about 2 medium oranges)
1 tablespoon vanilla extract
1 teaspoon ground cinnamon
½ teaspoon ground nutmeg

Preheat oven to 350°F.

Spray a 13 × 9 × 2-inch baking pan with vegetable oil spray. Put bread pieces in pan. Set aside.

In a large saucepan, heat milk, sugar, and cocoa powder over medium heat until sugar has dissolved and mixture looks like hot chocolate, about 3 minutes, whisking constantly.

Whisk in remaining ingredients. Pour over bread and let mixture sit for 15 minutes, or until bread has absorbed all the liquid.

Bake for 45 to 60 minutes, or until pudding is puffed up in center and a knife inserted in center comes out clean. Serve warm or cold.

COOK'S TIP ON CITRUS ZEST: Use a zester or kitchen rasp to get the top layer of citrus peel without also getting any of the white pith, which is bitter.

Calories 172
Protein 5 g
Carbohydrates 37 g
Fiber 2 g
Total Fat 1 g
  Saturated 1 g
  Polyunsaturated 0 g
  Monounsaturated 1 g
Cholesterol 1 mg
Sodium 181 mg

chocolate mini-soufflés

Soufflé success starts with organization. Do most of the steps in advance, whip your egg whites at the last minute, and pop the soufflés immediately into a hot oven.

Vegetable oil spray
1 tablespoon sugar
$^1/_2$ cup sugar
3 tablespoons cornstarch
3 to 4 tablespoons unsweetened cocoa powder (Dutch process preferred)
1 cup fat-free milk

2 tablespoons almond-, orange-, or chocolate-flavored liqueur (optional)
Whites of 4 large eggs
1 tablespoon sugar
$^1/_8$ teaspoon cream of tartar
30 semisweet chocolate chunks (about 1$^1/_2$ ounces)

Spray six 5- to 6-ounce custard cups or ramekins with vegetable oil spray. Spoon $^1/_2$ teaspoon sugar into each custard cup, tilting to lightly coat sides. Place cups on a rimmed baking sheet.

Sift $^1/_2$ cup sugar, cornstarch, and cocoa powder into a medium saucepan.

Whisk in milk (mixture will be slightly lumpy). Cook over medium-high heat for 4 to 6 minutes, or until mixture is thickened, whisking occasionally at first, then constantly when mixture starts to thicken. Remove from heat.

Stir in liqueur. Let stand for 5 minutes, stirring occasionally. (Mixture can be covered and refrigerated for up to two days. Let chilled mixture stand at room temperature for 10 minutes before folding into egg whites, below.)

Preheat oven to 400°F.

In a medium bowl, beat egg whites with an electric mixer on medium until eggs are foamy.

Add sugar and cream of tartar; beat on high until stiff peaks form. Using a rubber scraper, fold custard mixture into egg white mixture. Measure a heaping $^1/_2$ cup of mixture into each custard cup.

Place 5 chocolate pieces in middle of each cup, using a spoon to press chocolate down into mixture.

Bake for 10 to 11 minutes, or until centers are set (don't jiggle when soufflés are gently shaken). Place custard cups on plates and serve warm.

CHOCOLATE MINI-SOUFFLÉS

Calories 169
Protein 5 g
Carbohydrates 33 g
Fiber 1 g
Total Fat 2 g
  Saturated 1 g
  Polyunsaturated 0 g
  Monounsaturated 0 g
Cholesterol 1 mg
Sodium 60 mg

FROZEN CHOCOLATE MINI-SOUFFLÉS

To serve frozen, let soufflés cool, cover custard cups with aluminum foil, and freeze for at least 4 hours. Substitute 3 tablespoons mini chocolate chips (1½ teaspoons per serving) for the chocolate chunks; the chips are easier to bite into. The frozen soufflés will keep for about one month in the freezer.

chocolate rum sauce

SERVES 12; 2 TABLESPOONS PER SERVING

It's easy, it tastes great, and it's very versatile. You can make this sauce ahead of time and store it in the refrigerator, then use it warm or cold to dress up a dessert, such as nonfat frozen yogurt.

1 cup sugar	¼ cup light corn syrup
6 tablespoons light stick margarine	¼ cup white or dark rum or fruit-flavored liqueur
½ cup unsweetened cocoa powder	

In a medium saucepan, combine sugar and margarine; cook over medium heat until sugar has dissolved, about 5 minutes, stirring occasionally. Remove from heat.

Stir in remaining ingredients.

fudge icing

This super-rich icing is just the right topping for almost any layer cake or cupcake. We suggest trying it on Super Chocolaty Cake (page 78) or Pumpkin Spice Cake (page 18).

$\frac{3}{4}$ cup sugar

$\frac{3}{4}$ cup unsweetened cocoa powder (Dutch process preferred)

1   cup regular or mocha-flavor fat-free liquid nondairy creamer

$\frac{1}{3}$ cup reduced-fat semisweet chocolate chips

In a small saucepan, whisk together sugar, cocoa powder, and enough creamer (about $\frac{1}{3}$ cup) to make a thick paste. Add remaining creamer, whisking until blended. Bring to a boil over medium-high heat, whisking constantly. Reduce heat and simmer for 2 minutes. Remove from heat.

Stir in chocolate chips; whisk until chocolate melts. Transfer icing to a glass bowl, and place plastic wrap directly on surface. Refrigerate until thick and spreadable, about 30 minutes. Icing will keep stored like this or in an airtight plastic bag for up to three days in the refrigerator.

Calories 127
Protein 2 g
Carbohydrates 27 g
Fiber 1 g
Total Fat 1 g
 Saturated 1 g
 Polyunsaturated 0 g
 Monounsaturated 0 g
Cholesterol 0 mg
Sodium 3 mg

creamy
milk chocolate icing

MAKES 1½ CUPS ICING, ENOUGH FOR AN 8-INCH DOUBLE-LAYER CAKE,

AN 11 X 7 X 1½-INCH SHEET CAKE, OR 12 CUPCAKES

Try this wonderful frosting with your favorite low-fat white, yellow, chocolate, or sponge cake or as a filling between two cookies, even biscotti.

2 tablespoons fat-free tub margarine	¼ cup milk chocolate chips
½ cup sugar	3½ cups sifted confectioners' sugar
¼ cup plus 2 tablespoons fat-free milk	1 teaspoon vanilla extract

In a small saucepan, melt margarine over medium heat.

Whisk in sugar, milk, and chocolate chips. Cook for 3 minutes, or until smooth, whisking constantly. Transfer to a medium glass bowl and place plastic wrap directly on surface. Refrigerate for 15 minutes.

Whisk in confectioners' sugar and vanilla until blended.

Refrigerate for up to three days in a glass bowl with plastic wrap directly on surface or in an airtight plastic bag.

COOK'S TIP: Fifteen minutes is just the right amount of chilling time for this icing. If you chill it longer, whisking in the confectioners' sugar may be difficult; if you add the sugar while the mixture is still hot, the sugar will dissolve.

Calories 168
Protein 1 g
Carbohydrates 40 g
Fiber 0 g
Total Fat 1 g
  Saturated 1 g
  Polyunsaturated 0 g
  Monounsaturated 0 g
Cholesterol 1 mg
Sodium 22 mg

Fresh Fruit Trifle

Lime Fool with Raspberries and Kiwifruit

Tiramisù

Plum Good Clafouti

Crème Brûlée with Peaches

Mile-High Chilled Cranberry Soufflé

Frozen Gold Kiwifruit Soufflé

Coconut Flans with Dark Chocolate Sauce

Triple-Berry, Triple-Citrus Summer Pudding

Fruit-Laden Ricotta Ramekins

a spoonful of pudding

fresh fruit trifle

SERVES 8; ABOUT 1 CUP PER SERVING

Trifle is typically a dessert of layered sponge cake, custard, fruit, jam, sherry, and whipped cream. We deliciously lightened our version by using angel food cake, custard, and whipped topping that are fat free.

custard

½	cup sugar
3	tablespoons all-purpose flour
2	cups fat-free milk
	Egg substitute equivalent to 2 eggs, or 2 large eggs
2	teaspoons grated lemon zest
1	teaspoon vanilla extract

❖

2	tablespoons dry sherry or orange juice
2	tablespoons brandy or orange juice

6	cups cubed angel food cake (about ½ 9-inch cake)
½	cup all-fruit strawberry spread, warmed
1	quart fresh strawberries, halved (3 to 4 cups)
1	pint fresh blueberries (about 2 cups)
8	ounces frozen fat-free or light whipped topping, thawed
8	whole fresh strawberries
	Fresh mint sprigs (optional)

For custard, in a medium saucepan combine sugar and flour.

Whisk in remaining custard ingredients except vanilla. Cook over medium heat for 10 to 12 minutes, or until mixture thickens and coats a metal spoon, whisking constantly. Remove from heat.

Stir in vanilla. Let cool while beginning to assemble trifle.

In a small bowl, combine sherry and brandy.

To assemble, arrange half the cake cubes in a 1½- or 2-quart glass bowl. Drizzle with half the strawberry spread and half the sherry mixture. Place some halved strawberries around inside of bowl, cut side out and tips pointing up. Sprinkle half the blueberries over strawberry spread. Spoon half the custard over blueberries. Repeat, ending with custard. Spread whipped topping over custard. Cover with plastic wrap and refrigerate for 4 hours or overnight.

To serve, reach serving spoon through all layers to get all the different flavors and textures. Place each serving in a bowl or on a dessert plate, and garnish with a whole strawberry and fresh mint.

COOK'S TIP: Substitute a small package of sugar-free, fat-free (about 1 ounce) or regular (about 3.4 ounces) instant vanilla pudding, prepared with fat-free milk and the 2 teaspoons lemon zest, for the custard ingredients.

Calories 270
Protein 7 g
Carbohydrates 55 g
Fiber 1 g
Total Fat 1 g
 Saturated 0 g
 Polyunsaturated 0 g
 Monounsaturated 0 g
Cholesterol 1 mg
Sodium 133 mg

lime fool with raspberries and kiwifruit

Dating back to fifteenth-century England, fools are light desserts made with fruit and whipped cream. This fool is layered with fresh berries, kiwifruit, and a sweet yet tart lime-flavored yogurt mixture.

16 ounces plain fat-free yogurt without gelatin
2 cups fresh raspberries or sliced strawberries (1 pint)
2 tablespoons crème de cassis or other fruit liqueur (optional)

2 medium kiwifruit
2 tablespoons sugar
2 teaspoons finely shredded lime zest, divided use

Line a colander with two layers of cheesecloth or paper coffee filters. Put colander in a deep bowl (make sure colander doesn't touch bottom of bowl). Spoon yogurt into colander and refrigerate overnight; discard liquid (remaining solid is called yogurt cheese).

Several hours before serving, in a small bowl, gently stir together raspberries and liqueur. Let stand at room temperature for about 30 minutes; drain well.

Peel kiwifruit and cut each into 6 horizontal slices.

Stir together yogurt cheese, sugar, and 1 teaspoon lime zest.

To assemble, place a few raspberries in each of four wineglasses. Press 3 kiwifruit slices against inside of each glass. Spoon half the yogurt mixture into glasses. Spoon remaining berries over yogurt mixture. Top with remaining yogurt mixture. Sprinkle with remaining lime zest. Cover and refrigerate for 1 to 2 hours before serving.

COOK'S TIP ON YOGURT CHEESE: For the consistency you want in yogurt cheese, use yogurt that contains no gelatin. Gelatin holds in the whey, or liquid, keeping you from getting a thick, creamy end product.

Calories 121
Protein 5 g
Carbohydrates 25 g
Fiber 6 g
Total Fat 1 g
  Saturated 0 g
  Polyunsaturated 0 g
  Monounsaturated 0 g
Cholesterol 2 mg
Sodium 45 mg

tiramisù

You've had it at your favorite Italian restaurant, and now you can have tiramisù at home. It's easy to put together and tastes delectable.

8   ounces nonfat or light sour cream (about 1 cup)
½   cup unsifted confectioners' sugar
3   ounces reduced-fat cream cheese (not fat-free)
1   teaspoon vanilla extract
8   ounces frozen fat-free or light whipped topping, thawed (about 3 cups)

9   ladyfingers
¼   cup strong cold coffee
¼   cup coffee-flavored liqueur, or ¼ cup coffee plus 2 tablespoons sugar
1   to 2 tablespoons unsweetened cocoa powder

In a medium mixing bowl, beat sour cream, confectioners' sugar, cream cheese, and vanilla with an electric mixer on medium until smooth.

Using a rubber scraper, fold in whipped topping until well blended.

Break ladyfingers into bite-size pieces; arrange half in an 8-inch square baking pan.

In a small bowl, stir together coffee and liqueur.

To assemble, drizzle half the coffee mixture over ladyfingers. Spoon half the sour cream mixture evenly on top, then sprinkle with half the cocoa powder. Repeat. Cover with plastic wrap and refrigerate for 8 to 48 hours.

COOK'S TIP ON COCOA POWDER: For even distribution, use a fine-mesh strainer to sprinkle cocoa powder.

Calories 175
Protein 3 g
Carbohydrates 29 g
Fiber 0 g
Total Fat 3 g
  Saturated 2 g
  Polyunsaturated 0 g
  Monounsaturated 1 g
Cholesterol 35 mg
Sodium 83 mg

low-fat & luscious desserts

plum good clafouti

After a summer meal, tempt your taste buds with wedges of this custardy dessert.
When you want a change from plums, substitute pitted cherries, peaches, apricots, or even grapes.

1 pound fresh plums, sliced (5 to 8 medium)	1 teaspoon vanilla extract
2 tablespoons sugar	1/8 teaspoon salt
1 tablespoon almond-flavored liqueur or 1/2 teaspoon almond extract	1/2 cup all-purpose flour
Vegetable oil spray	1 cup fat-free milk
Egg substitute equivalent to 3 eggs	2 tablespoons light stick margarine, melted
1/2 cup sugar	1 tablespoon light brown sugar

In a medium bowl, combine plums, 2 tablespoons sugar, and liqueur. Cover and let stand at room temperature for 15 to 30 minutes (the longer plums stand, the juicier they get).

Preheat oven to 400°F. Spray a 9-inch round cake pan with vegetable oil spray. Set aside.

In a medium bowl, whisk together egg substitute, 1/2 cup sugar, vanilla, and salt. Whisk in flour until combined (batter may be slightly lumpy).

In a small bowl, whisk together milk and margarine; gradually whisk into flour mixture until combined.

Arrange fruit in a circular pattern on bottom of cake pan; pour any remaining juice over fruit. Pour batter over fruit, then sprinkle with brown sugar.

Bake for 15 minutes; reduce oven temperature to 350°F and bake for 30 to 35 minutes, or until a knife inserted in center comes out clean. Let cool for at least 10 minutes on a cooling rack. Serve warm.

COOK'S TIP ON MACERATING FRUIT: When fruit is allowed to soak, or macerate, in a flavored liquid, often a liqueur, the fruit absorbs the flavor much as meat absorbs the flavor of a marinade. A tasty combination for 1 pound of fruit is 1 to 2 tablespoons fruit juice, such as orange juice, mixed with 1/8 to 1/4 teaspoon each cinnamon and nutmeg and 1/4 to 1/2 teaspoon grated citrus zest.

Calories 167
Protein 5 g
Carbohydrates 33 g
Fiber 1 g
Total Fat 2 g
  Saturated 0 g
  Polyunsaturated 1 g
  Monounsaturated 1 g
Cholesterol 1 mg
Sodium 119 mg

crème brûlée
with peaches

If you want an impressive make-ahead dessert, try this striking treat. It's a combination of creamy white custard and fresh peaches, blanketed in a rich, dark sugar glaze.

Vegetable oil spray

custard
2 cups fat-free milk
Egg substitute equivalent to 3 eggs,
or 3 large eggs
$\frac{1}{3}$ cup sugar

Whites of 2 large eggs
$1\frac{1}{2}$ teaspoons vanilla extract

❖

1 large peach or nectarine
$\frac{1}{4}$ cup plus 2 tablespoons firmly packed dark brown sugar

Preheat oven 350°F. Spray six 5- to 6-ounce custard cups or ramekins with vegetable oil spray. Set aside.

For custard, in a small saucepan, heat milk over medium-high heat until tiny bubbles begin to form around edges, about 7 minutes (no stirring needed). Don't allow milk to come to a boil.

Meanwhile, in a medium bowl, combine remaining custard ingredients except vanilla, stirring well with a fork (don't use a whisk).

When milk is hot, very slowly pour it into egg mixture, stirring constantly with a fork. (Adding milk too quickly may cause eggs to curdle.)

Stir in vanilla. Spoon mixture into custard cups.

Arrange custard cups in a 13 × 9 × 2-inch baking pan, place in oven, and pour about 4 cups hot tap water into baking pan.

Bake for 45 minutes, or until knife inserted in center comes out clean. Remove custard cups from baking pan and let cool completely on cooling rack. Cover custard cups with plastic wrap and refrigerate until needed, preferably overnight.

At serving time, preheat broiler.

Peel peach; cut into 18 slices. Decoratively arrange 3 slices on each serving of custard; sprinkle each serving with 1 tablespoon brown sugar. Place custard cups on baking sheet and broil 2 to 3 inches from heat for about 2 minutes, or until sugar melts, being careful not to let it burn. Let stand for 5 minutes, then serve. (If allowed to sit for long, sugar will break down and melt into custard rather than staying on top.)

Calories 154
Protein 7 g
Carbohydrates 31 g
Fiber 0 g
Total Fat 0 g
  Saturated 0 g
  Polyunsaturated 0 g
  Monounsaturated 0 g
Cholesterol 2 mg
Sodium 116 mg

german chocolate cake with pecan coconut frosting *(page 80)*

apple cinnamon cake *(page 22)*

chocolate orange bread pudding with
chocolate rum sauce *(pages 97 and 99)*

"hamburger" cake *(page 12)*

brandy orange snaps, pecan-pie cookies, and
gingerbread window cookies *(pages 37, 32, and 44)*

chocolate walnut brownies and lemony lime squares
(pages 92 and 48)

granola bar pie with pretzel crust *(page 54)*

tropical fruit pie *(page 60)*

mixed berry tart with apricot glaze *(page 64)*   summertime peach tart *(page 63)*

frozen turtle pie *(page 58)*

cheesecake with fresh berry sauce *(page 26)*

mile-high chilled cranberry soufflé

SERVES 10; 3/4 TO 1 CUP PER SERVING

Although it is light, this really tall dessert is sturdier than its baked cousins. Make it early in the day so it has adequate time to chill. For a more subdued look, use a larger soufflé dish or spoon individual portions into martini glasses, parfait glasses, small ramekins, or custard cups before refrigerating.

2 cups fresh or frozen whole cranberries, picked over (about 8 ounces)

1 1/2 cups cranberry juice cocktail

1/2 to 3/4 cup sugar

2 envelopes unflavored gelatin (2 tablespoons)
Whites of 4 large eggs, room temperature

1/2 cup sugar

1 tablespoon plus 1 teaspoon water

1/4 teaspoon cream of tartar

2 cups frozen fat-free or light whipped topping, thawed (about 5 ounces)
Frozen fat-free or light whipped topping, thawed, or whole cranberries (optional)

To make a collar for a 1-quart soufflé dish, measure a 12-inch piece of aluminum foil and fold in half lengthwise. Wrap foil around outside of dish, overlapping ends by about 2 inches and extending foil about 4 inches above rim. Fasten securely with cellophane tape or a tight-fitting rubber band. Set aside.

In a medium saucepan, combine cranberries, cranberry juice cocktail, and 1/2 to 3/4 cup sugar. Place over medium-high heat and sprinkle with gelatin, stirring constantly. Cook until gelatin and sugar have dissolved and cranberries pop, 8 to 10 minutes, stirring occasionally. Let mixture cool for about 10 minutes, then refrigerate until partially jelled to the consistency of jam, about 2 hours. (If mixture jells too long, stir until desired consistency is reached.)

Combine remaining ingredients except whipped topping in top of a double boiler over simmering water (water shouldn't touch bottom of pan). Cook over very low heat, beating constantly with a handheld electric mixer on low until mixture reaches 160°F on a candy or instant-read thermometer, about 15 minutes (you can use a rotary beater or whisk, but it will take longer). Transfer to a large bowl and beat on medium-high until very stiff peaks form.

With a rubber scraper, gently fold in cranberry mixture and whipped topping until just incorporated. Spoon carefully into soufflé dish. Refrigerate for at least 4 hours, or until soufflé is well chilled and firmly set. Remove foil collar. Garnish with a decorative dollop of whipped topping or a few cranberries.

Calories 154
Protein 3 g
Carbohydrates 35 g
Fiber 1 g
Total Fat 0 g
  Saturated 0 g
  Polyunsaturated 0 g
  Monounsaturated 0 g
Cholesterol 0 mg
Sodium 34 mg

frozen gold kiwifruit soufflé

SERVES 10; ABOUT 3/4 CUP PER SERVING

Lovely for Mother's Day and summer celebrations!
This pale yellow frozen soufflé is the perfect blend of sweet and tart flavors.

Vegetable oil spray

3 gold or green kiwifruit, peeled and sliced

2 tablespoons lemon juice (fresh preferred)

½ cup cold water

2 envelopes unflavored gelatin
(2 tablespoons)

1 cup sugar

1 cup water

⅓ cup powdered egg whites (pasteurized dried egg whites)

½ teaspoon vanilla extract

12 ounces frozen fat-free or light whipped topping, thawed (about 4½ cups)

1 gold kiwifruit (optional)

To make a collar for a 2-quart soufflé dish, measure a piece of aluminum foil long enough to go around the dish plus about 2 inches; fold in half lengthwise. Spray dish and one side of foil with vegetable oil spray. Wrap foil, sprayed side in, around outside of dish at upper edge, overlapping ends by about 2 inches and extending foil about 3 inches above rim. Fasten securely with cellophane tape or a tight-fitting rubber band. Set aside.

In a food processor or blender, puree kiwifruit and lemon juice. Set aside.

Pour ½ cup cold water into a medium saucepan. Sprinkle gelatin on water and let soften, about 3 minutes. Cook over low heat until gelatin dissolves, 3 to 4 minutes, stirring occasionally. Stir in reserved kiwi mixture (mixture will be very thin); refrigerate.

In a large mixing bowl, stir together sugar, 1 cup water, powdered egg whites, and vanilla. Beat with an electric mixer on high until stiff peaks form. Using a rubber scraper, fold kiwi mixture gently but thoroughly into egg white mixture for several minutes. (Ingredients will seem combined sooner, but very thorough folding is necessary to prevent separating and settling during freezing.)

Fold in whipped topping until mixture is thoroughly blended. Pour into soufflé dish, smoothing top with rubber scraper. Freeze for 3 hours or overnight.

To serve, slice remaining kiwi and decorate top of soufflé. Spoon into individual dessert bowls or stemmed glassware.

Calories 169
Protein 4 g
Carbohydrates 35 g
Fiber 1 g
Total Fat 0 g
 Saturated 0 g
 Polyunsaturated 0 g
 Monounsaturated 0 g
Cholesterol 0 mg
Sodium 67 mg

COOK'S TIP ON POWDERED EGG WHITES AND MERINGUE POWDER: Powdered egg whites, also called pasteurized dried egg whites, are available in supermarkets, usually near the powdered and evaporated milk. They provide a safe way to enjoy egg whites in unbaked desserts—no worry about salmonella from unpasteurized eggs. Simply add water and beat with an electric mixer. Meringue powder is similar but contains sugar. Look for it in gourmet shops and party supply stores.

COOK'S TIP ON GOLD KIWIFRUIT: Available from June through September, gold kiwifruit are sweeter than the more familiar green kiwifruit. Both have edible black seeds and are brown on the outside, but the gold variety isn't fuzzy.

coconut flans with dark chocolate sauce

SERVES 8; 1 FLAN AND 1 GENEROUS TABLESPOON SAUCE PER SERVING

To intensify the coconut flavor in this unusual dessert, you steep the coconut in milk, strain and squeeze it dry, then discard it, using only the remaining flavored milk. Deep, dark chocolate sauce is the decadent-tasting topping.

flans

2 1/2	cups fat-free milk
1	cup sweetened flaked coconut
	Egg substitute equivalent to 3 eggs
1/2	cup sugar
1	tablespoon cornstarch
1	to 1 1/2 teaspoons coconut extract
1/2	teaspoon vanilla extract

❖

Vegetable oil spray

sauce

1/4	cup plus 1 tablespoon water
1/4	cup sugar
1	tablespoon dark corn syrup
3	tablespoons unsweetened cocoa powder (Dutch process preferred)
1/2	teaspoon vanilla extract
1/2	teaspoon chocolate extract

For flans, in a medium saucepan, stir together milk and coconut. Bring to a simmer over medium-high heat; turn off heat and let steep for 15 minutes. Remove from burner. Drain in a strainer over a medium bowl, retaining milk. Press against strainer until coconut is as dry as possible; discard coconut. Return milk to saucepan and bring to a simmer over medium heat.

In a small bowl, whisk together egg substitute, sugar, and cornstarch. Whisk egg mixture into hot milk in saucepan.

Whisk in extracts.

Preheat oven to 300°F.

Spray eight 5- to 6-ounce custard cups or ramekins with vegetable oil spray. Carefully pour about 1/3 cup milk mixture into each. Arrange cups in a large baking pan, with a rim, place in oven, and pour 1 inch of boiling water into large pan.

Bake for 30 to 35 minutes, or until custards are just set. (Centers should jiggle when you shake pan.) Let cool on a cooling rack until room temperature, about 30 minutes.

Meanwhile, for sauce, whisk together water, sugar, and corn syrup in a small saucepan. Cook over medium heat until mixture comes to a boil, whisking constantly. Boil for 1 minute; remove from heat.

Calories 148
Protein 5 g
Carbohydrates 28 g
Fiber 1 g
Total Fat 1 g
  Saturated 1 g
  Polyunsaturated 0 g
  Monounsaturated 0 g
Cholesterol 1 mg
Sodium 90 mg

Add cocoa powder, whisking until smooth.

Whisk in vanilla and chocolate extracts. Cover and refrigerate for at least 1 hour.

To serve, use a knife to loosen edges of flans and invert onto serving dish or individual dessert platter; spoon sauce over each flan.

triple-berry, triple-citrus summer pudding

SERVES 6; ½ CUP PLUS 2 TABLESPOONS WHIPPED TOPPING PER SERVING

Similar to a wonderful chilled bread pudding, summer pudding is very popular in the British Isles. This one pairs the zest and juice of three kinds of citrus with a trio of plump, juicy berries. Simply delicious!

Vegetable oil spray
3 slices potato bread
1 small lemon
1 small lime
1 small orange
½ cup sugar
1 cup fresh raspberries or frozen lightly sweetened raspberries (½ pint fresh or 10 ounces frozen

1 cup fresh or frozen unsweetened blueberries (½ pint fresh or about 6 ounces frozen)
1 cup fresh or frozen unsweetened blackberries (½ pint fresh or about 8 ounces frozen)
1 tablespoon orange-flavored liqueur
⅔ cup frozen fat-free or light whipped topping, thawed

Preheat oven to 250°F. Spray six 5- to 6-ounce custard cups or ramekins with vegetable oil spray.

Remove crusts from bread; discard crusts. Cut bread into ½-inch cubes (you should have about 2 cups). Put cubes on an ungreased baking sheet.

Bake for 15 to 20 minutes, or until bread is dry but not browned. Let bread cool for at least 10 minutes.

Meanwhile, grate ½ teaspoon zest each from lemon, lime, and orange, keeping orange zest separate from others. Set aside. Squeeze 1 teaspoon juice from each into a medium saucepan, then stir in sugar.

Gently stir all berries into sugar mixture. Bring to a simmer over medium-high heat; reduce heat to medium-low and cook for 5 minutes (6 to 7 minutes if using frozen berries), gently shaking and tilting pan occasionally to help dissolve sugar without breaking up berries. Remove from heat.

Gently stir in lemon zest, lime zest, and liqueur. Let cool for 15 minutes.

Calories 150
Protein 4 g
Carbohydrates 35 g
Fiber 4 g
Total Fat 1 g
  Saturated 0 g
  Polyunsaturated 0 g
  Monounsaturated 0 g
Cholesterol 0 mg
Sodium 60 mg

Place custard cups on a rimmed baking sheet. Spoon a scant $\frac{1}{4}$ cup berry mixture into each cup. Top each with a single layer of bread cubes. Repeat. Loosely cover each cup with plastic wrap. Place a weight, such as an 8-ounce can of tomato sauce, on each. Refrigerate for 6 to 24 hours.

In a small bowl, combine whipped topping and reserved orange zest. Cover and refrigerate until ready to use.

To serve, remove weights and plastic wrap from pudding. Run a thin spatula or thin, sharp knife around inside of cups to release pudding. Invert each pudding onto a plate. Spoon 2 tablespoons whipped topping onto each pudding.

COOK'S TIP: You can prepare the berry mixture up to two days in advance, then layer it with the bread, weight it, and refrigerate it for 6 to 24 hours before you plan to serve the dessert.

COOK'S TIP ON CLEANING BERRIES: The best way to clean fresh berries without breaking them is to fill a bowl with cold water and soak the berries for 15 to 20 seconds. Drain and repeat with clean water.

fruit-laden ricotta ramekins

A cross between a soufflé and bread pudding, these ramekins should be served warm. Although their size is dainty, they are filling and flavorful.

Butter-flavor vegetable oil spray
2 teaspoons sugar (about) for coating ramekins
1½ cups water
3 tablespoons creamed wheat cereal granules (farina), uncooked
1 15-ounce container fat-free or low-fat ricotta cheese
¼ cup plus 1 tablespoon firmly packed confectioners' sugar

Whites of 2 large eggs
1½ teaspoons vanilla extract
½ to ¾ cup dried currants
2 tablespoons crème de cassis
White of 1 large egg
½ cup frozen fat-free or light whipped topping, thawed (optional)

Preheat oven to 375°F. Spray eight 3-ounce ramekins or custard cups with vegetable oil spray. With a paper towel, gently wipe each ramekin to remove excess spray. Sprinkle sugar in ramekins and swirl to coat bottoms and sides. Tap each ramekin on a flat surface to loosen excess sugar; discard excess sugar.

In a small saucepan over high heat, bring water to a boil. Gradually stir cereal into boiling water. Reduce heat and let simmer for 3 minutes (mixture will be slightly watery). Set aside to cool for 15 to 20 minutes.

In a food processor or blender, process ricotta until smooth.

Add confectioners' sugar, 2 egg whites, and vanilla; process until blended.

Add cooled cereal; process until smooth. Transfer mixture back to saucepan or to a large bowl; stir in currants and crème de cassis.

In a small mixing bowl, with an electric mixer on medium, beat remaining egg white until stiff. With a rubber scraper, gently fold it into ricotta mixture. Gently spoon into ramekins; place ramekins on a baking sheet.

Bake for 35 to 40 minutes, or until puffy and lightly browned (ramekins will deflate slightly when removed from oven). Top each serving with a dollop of whipped topping.

Calories 130
Protein 9 g
Carbohydrates 21 g
Fiber 1 g
Total Fat 0 g
  Saturated 0 g
  Polyunsaturated 0 g
  Monounsaturated 0 g
Cholesterol 4 mg
Sodium 126 mg

Replace the currants with small bits of your favorite dried fruits, substituting a different liqueur if you like. For example, dried apricots and orange-flavored liqueur marry nicely. For a change from whipped topping, try a sprinkling of sifted unsweetened cocoa powder or a few shavings of semisweet chocolate. You can even replace the fruit with reduced-fat chocolate bits.

Pistachio Orange Cream with Berries

Honey Almond Cream with Berries

Sweet-Spiced Fruit with Cabernet Sauce

Mimosa Fruit

Mango Mixup

Wine-Poached Pears with Vanilla Sauce

Berries Brûlée

Winter Fruit Compote

Caramelized Nectarines

Roasted Fresh Peaches with Pistachio Stuffing

Blueberry Kissel

Oranges in Caramel

Clementines in Caramel

fruit, lover's basket of treats

pistachio orange cream with berries

SERVES 12; $^1/_3$ CUP BERRIES AND 2 TABLESPOONS ORANGE CREAM PER SERVING

A low-fat cousin of classic cannoli cream filling, this version combines orange, pistachio, and a touch of chocolate. Serve it over a mixture of fresh raspberries, strawberries, and blueberries.

1 cup no-salt-added 1 percent cottage cheese	$^1/_2$ pint fresh raspberries (about 1 cup)
$^1/_2$ cup nonfat or light sour cream	$^1/_2$ pint fresh blueberries (about 1 cup)
$^1/_2$ cup all-fruit orange marmalade or no-sugar-added orange marmalade	$^1/_4$ cup miniature semisweet chocolate chips
2 tablespoons confectioners' sugar	$^1/_4$ cup shelled unsalted pistachios, dry-roasted and coarsely chopped (see Cook's Tip on Dry-Roasting Nuts, page 68)
1 teaspoon orange-flavored liqueur (optional)	
1 pint fresh strawberries (about 2 cups)	

In a food processor or blender, process cottage cheese for 1 minute. Scrape sides of container and process for 1 minute, or until smooth. Transfer to an airtight container; refrigerate for about 8 hours, or until firm.

Put cottage cheese in a medium bowl; gently fold in sour cream.

Fold in marmalade, confectioners' sugar, and liqueur (at this point, mixture can be refrigerated for up to two days in an airtight container).

At serving time, slice strawberries; in a medium bowl, gently combine with other berries. Spoon about $^1/_3$ cup berries into each of 12 individual bowls or goblets. Top each serving with about 2 tablespoons orange cream mixture, then sprinkle with about 1 teaspoon each of chocolate chips and nuts.

HONEY ALMOND CREAM WITH BERRIES

Follow directions above to cream cottage cheese and fold in sour cream. Replace marmalade, sugar, and liqueur with $^1/_4$ cup honey and $^1/_2$ teaspoon almond extract; replace chocolate chips and pistachios with $^1/_2$ cup slivered almonds, dry-roasted.

PISTACHIO ORANGE CREAM WITH BERRIES

Calories 112
Protein 4 g
Carbohydrates 19 g
Fiber 3 g
Total Fat 3 g
 Saturated 1 g
 Polyunsaturated 0 g
 Monounsaturated 1 g
Cholesterol 3 mg
Sodium 21 mg

HONEY ALMOND CREAM WITH BERRIES

Calories 96
Protein 4 g
Carbohydrates 14 g
Fiber 2 g
Total Fat 3 g
 Saturated 0 g
 Polyunsaturated 1 g
 Monounsaturated 2 g
Cholesterol 3 mg
Sodium 22 mg

low-fat & luscious desserts

sweet-spiced fruit with cabernet sauce

SERVES 4; ABOUT $^2/_3$ CUP PER SERVING

Cinnamon, cloves, and fresh ginger flavor a ruby-red wine reduction that cradles oranges and star fruit or kiwifruit. The sauce also complements other fruit, such as pear or apple slices or a combination of honeydew and watermelon cubes.

cabernet sauce

2 cups cabernet sauvignon or other dry red wine (regular or nonalcoholic)

$^1/_4$ cup sugar

4 cinnamon sticks, each about 3 inches long

8 whole cloves

1 teaspoon grated gingerroot

❖

2 medium navel oranges, peeled and sectioned

2 star fruit, each cut into 8 slices, or 2 medium kiwifruit, peeled and each cut into 8 wedges or slices

For sauce, in a medium saucepan, combine ingredients except gingerroot. Bring to a boil over high heat; boil without stirring for 9 minutes, or until mixture has reduced to $^1/_2$ cup. Remove from heat and let cool completely, 15 to 20 minutes. Remove cinnamon sticks and cloves.

Stir in gingerroot.

To serve, spoon 2 tablespoons sauce onto each of four dessert plates. Decoratively arrange fruit on sauce.

COOK'S TIP: To prepare the sauce ahead of time, follow the directions above, but cover and refrigerate it after removing the cinnamon sticks and cloves. To serve, reheat the sauce over medium-low heat for 1 to 2 minutes, or until sauce reaches a thin consistency, then stir in gingerroot. Arrange the sauce and the fruit as directed above.

COOK'S TIP ON CUTTING CITRUS FRUIT: Here's an easy way to get rid of the bitter white pith when removing the peel from citrus fruit. Cut a thin slice from the top and the bottom of a piece of the fruit. Next, remove the remaining peel in vertical slices. Slice or section the fruit, and you'll have pretty pieces.

Calories 141*
Protein 1 g
Carbohydrates 29 g
Fiber 5 g
Total Fat 0 g
  Saturated 0 g
  Polyunsaturated 0 g
  Monounsaturated 0 g
Cholesterol 0 mg
Sodium 7 mg

*Estimated based on loss of alcohol during reduction of sauce.

mimosa fruit

Imagine summer fruits served icy cold in frozen goblets and drenched with bubbly sweetened orange juice. Perfect for warm-weather brunches, hot nights, and everything in between.

2   cups fresh watermelon cubes
1   cup fresh honeydew cubes
½   cup fresh blueberries
½   cup frozen orange juice concentrate, thawed

1   tablespoon plus 1½ teaspoons sugar
1   cup diet or regular ginger ale or Champagne

In a medium bowl, gently stir fruit together. Divide evenly among four wine goblets. Put in freezer for 30 minutes.

Meanwhile, in a small bowl, stir together orange juice and sugar until sugar has dissolved.

To serve, spoon 2 tablespoons orange juice mixture into each goblet. Pour ¼ cup ginger ale over each serving. Serve immediately.

COOK'S TIP: You can cut the fruit as much as 8 hours in advance. Refrigerate each kind in a separate bowl, covered with plastic wrap. Combine gently, then arrange in goblets and place in freezer for 30 minutes before serving, as directed above.

Calories 120
Protein 1 g
Carbohydrates 32 g
Fiber 2 g
Total Fat 0 g
  Saturated 0 g
  Polyunsaturated 0 g
  Monounsaturated 0 g
Cholesterol 0 mg
Sodium 18 mg

mango mixup

Fresh mint takes center stage in this recipe. It does wonderful things to already luscious mangoes.

2 tablespoons fresh lemon juice
1 1/2 teaspoons sugar

2 medium mangoes, cubed (about 1 1/3 cups)
2 tablespoons chopped fresh mint leaves

In a medium mixing bowl, stir together lemon juice and sugar until sugar has dissolved.

Stir in mangoes, then gently stir in mint leaves.

COOK'S TIP: If fresh mint isn't available, try about 1/2 teaspoon grated gingerroot instead.

COOK'S TIP ON MANGOES: When purchasing mangoes, look for skins that are unblemished and turning yellow with red mottling. To ripen the fruit, place it in a paper bag at room temperature for 24 to 48 hours, or until fairly soft to the touch. Ripe mangoes can be refrigerated for about five days.

Calories 77
Protein 1 g
Carbohydrates 20 g
Fiber 2 g
Total Fat 0 g
 Saturated 0 g
 Polyunsaturated 0 g
 Monounsaturated 0 g
Cholesterol 0 mg
Sodium 4 mg

wine-poached pears with vanilla sauce

SERVES 6; 1 PEAR AND $1/4$ CUP SAUCE PER SERVING

Two toppings—one a thick red wine sauce, the other a creamy vanilla sauce—really dress up these burgundy-colored poached pears. Keep the vanilla sauce on hand to serve over fresh fruit or a cobbler, crisp, or cake.

pear mixture

6	medium Bosc or Bartlett pears
$1/2$	cup sugar
$3 1/2$	cups burgundy or other dry red wine (regular or nonalcoholic)
1	cup ruby port
1	stick cinnamon, about 3 inches long
6	cardamom seeds, lightly crushed
1	star anise

vanilla sauce

$1 1/2$	cups fat-free milk
	Egg substitute equivalent to 1 egg, or yolk of 1 large egg, lightly beaten
3	tablespoons sugar
1	tablespoon cornstarch
1	teaspoon vanilla extract

For pear mixture, peel pears and trim bottoms so pears will stand up. Set pears upright in a large saucepan and sprinkle with sugar.

Add remaining pear mixture ingredients. Cover and bring to a simmer over low heat; cook until pears are tender, 35 to 40 minutes. Transfer pears to a serving bowl, retaining poaching liquid in saucepan.

Meanwhile, for vanilla sauce, whisk together all ingredients except vanilla in a medium saucepan. Cook over medium heat for 5 to 10 minutes, or until mixture thickens to about consistency of heavy cream, whisking constantly. Remove from heat.

Whisk in vanilla.

Boil poaching liquid over high heat until it is reduced to 1 cup, about 5 minutes. Strain resulting syrup to remove spices; pour over pears.

Serve at room temperature or chilled. Spoon vanilla sauce over each serving.

COOK'S TIP ON CARDAMOM: A member of the ginger family, cardamom has a sweet, pungent aroma and a sweet, spicy flavor. Ground cardamom loses its flavor quickly, so it is better to buy the pods or the seeds. If using the seeds, leave them whole or grind them with a mortar and pestle, coffee grinder, or spice mill.

Calories 270*
Protein 4 g
Carbohydrates 59 g
Fiber 4 g
Total Fat 1 g
  Saturated 0 g
  Polyunsaturated 0 g
  Monounsaturated 0 g
Cholesterol 1 mg
Sodium 63 mg

*Estimated based on loss of alcohol during reduction of liquid.

COOK'S TIP ON STAR ANISE: The star-shaped, dark brown pod that gives star anise its name contains seeds commonly used to flavor tea, liqueurs, and baked goods. Similar in flavor but unrelated to anise, star anise can be found in the Asian section of large supermarkets and in Asian food markets. It is one of the ingredients in five-spice powder.

berries brûlée

This is a very simple and quick dessert to make when berries are in season. If you prefer, you can use any other soft fruit, such as sliced apricots, nectarines, or peaches, instead.

$^1/_2$ pint fresh blueberries (about 1 cup)

$^1/_2$ pint fresh raspberries (about 1 cup)

$^1/_2$ cup nonfat or light sour cream

$^1/_2$ cup firmly packed light brown sugar

Preheat broiler.

Divide berries evenly among six 5- to 6-ounce custard cups, ramekins, or broilerproof dessert bowls.

Spread sour cream evenly over berries, then sprinkle with brown sugar.

Broil about 4 inches from heat for 2 minutes, or until sugar melts. (If you have a kitchen blowtorch, you can use it, following manufacturer's directions carefully.)

COOK'S TIP: You can assemble, cover, and refrigerate this dessert up to 8 hours before broiling and serving it.

Calories 116
Protein 2 g
Carbohydrates 28 g
Fiber 2 g
Total Fat 0 g
 Saturated 0 g
 Polyunsaturated 0 g
 Monounsaturated 0 g
Cholesterol 2 mg
Sodium 25 mg

winter fruit compote

Serve this versatile warm fruit compote alone, or try it as an accompaniment to meats, as the filling for blintzes or crepes, or over fat-free vanilla ice cream or frozen yogurt.

8 ounces dried apricots (about 1⅓ cups)
1 cup dried cranberries
6 ounces dried peaches (about 1 cup)
4 ounces pitted prunes (about ⅔ cup)
3 mango tea bags or 1 tablespoon plus 1½ teaspoons loose mango tea in a tea ball
¾ cup firmly packed light brown sugar

Grated zest and juice of 2 medium oranges (navel preferred)
½ cup orange-flavored liqueur or juice of 1 medium orange (navel preferred)
1 cinnamon stick, about 3 inches long
¼ teaspoon freshly grated or ground nutmeg
¼ teaspoon minced gingerroot
⅛ teaspoon ground cloves

In a large glass bowl, combine apricots, cranberries, peaches, prunes, and tea bags; cover with lukewarm water. Cover bowl with plastic wrap or lid and let soak overnight.

Drain mixture in a colander, discarding tea bags and liquid. Transfer fruit mixture to a large saucepan and add remaining ingredients. Gently combine with a large rubber scraper so mixture is well blended but fruit remains intact. Bring to a low boil over medium heat. Reduce heat and simmer for 45 to 55 minutes, or until all fruit is soft.

Serve warm.

VARIATION

Go monochromatic and make this a red compote for the holidays. Soak dried cherries or cranberries, dried apples, and dried apricots with your favorite flavored tea (brewed tea or water with tea bags) and 3 to 4 cups (whatever you have left over) juice from freshly cooked beets. The important thing is to cover all the fruit with liquid; use lukewarm water to make up the difference. Soak overnight and drain the next day as directed above.

Calories 340
Protein 2 g
Carbohydrates 80 g
Fiber 7 g
Total Fat 1 g
  Saturated 0 g
  Polyunsaturated 0 g
  Monounsaturated 0 g
Cholesterol 0 mg
Sodium 14 mg

caramelized nectarines

This luscious dessert showcases fresh nectarines, which now, thanks to imports, are available year-round. Serve it over angel food cake or vanilla fat-free frozen yogurt.

4   large, firm but ripe nectarines or peaches (about 1¾ pounds)

1   teaspoon ground cinnamon
½   cup sugar

Cut nectarines into ½-inch slices; put in a medium bowl and stir in cinnamon.

To make caramel, in a large, heavy skillet, heat sugar over medium heat until melted and golden brown, 10 to 12 minutes, stirring frequently with a wooden spoon.

Add nectarines (caramel will harden). Cook until caramel has dissolved and nectarines are tender, about 5 minutes, stirring occasionally. Remove from heat; let cool for 5 minutes before serving.

COOK'S TIP ON CARAMELIZING: Making caramel is easy but needs a watchful eye. Use a heavy skillet to avoid scorching the caramel. The sugar will first clump, then melt and turn golden brown. Caramel is extremely hot, so take care when stirring.

COOK'S TIP ON NECTARINES: If your nectarines are not ripe, store them in a paper bag at room temperature for one or two days.

Calories 179
Protein 2 g
Carbohydrates 45 g
Fiber 3 g
Total Fat 1 g
  Saturated 0 g
  Polyunsaturated 0 g
  Monounsaturated 0 g
Cholesterol 0 mg
Sodium 0 mg

roasted fresh peaches with pistachio stuffing

SERVES 12; 1 LARGE PEACH HALF OR 2 SMALL PEACH HALVES PER SERVING

Elegant but easy to prepare, these unusual peaches should be served warm from the oven.

¾ cup crushed almond biscotti (about 3 large cookies)

½ cup shelled unsalted pistachios, finely chopped

¼ cup plus 2 tablespoons firmly packed light brown sugar

¼ teaspoon Chinese five-spice powder

1 large egg, lightly beaten (not egg substitute)

6 large or 12 small fresh peaches (almost too ripe), halved

½ cup water

¾ cup frozen fat-free or light whipped topping, thawed, or heavy Greek yogurt (optional)

Preheat oven to 350°F.

In a small bowl, stir together biscotti, pistachios, brown sugar, and five-spice powder.

Stir in egg. Spoon stuffing into peach halves and place them in two 13 × 9 × 2-inch baking pans or on two rimmed baking sheets. Carefully pour water around peaches.

Bake, uncovered, for 30 to 40 minutes, or until peaches are tender, checking after about 20 minutes to better estimate cooking time.

Top each serving with a dollop of whipped topping.

COOK'S TIP: Cooking time will vary with the size and ripeness of the peaches, but whether they are white-fleshed or yellow won't have any effect.

COOK'S TIP ON UNSALTED PISTACHIOS: If you can't find unsalted pistachios, rinse the salted variety and dry the nuts on a baking sheet lined with paper towels before chopping the nuts.

Calories 119
Protein 3 g
Carbohydrates 20 g
Fiber 2 g
Total Fat 4 g
  Saturated 1 g
  Polyunsaturated 1 g
  Monounsaturated 2 g
Cholesterol 19 mg
Sodium 25 mg

blueberry kissel

This easy dessert is prettiest when served in a glass bowl or a stemmed glass compote. Traditional in Russia, where blueberries abound in the summertime, kissel is a sweetened, thickened fruit puree. Instead of using whipped topping, you can crown this dessert with custard sauce if you prefer.

4 cups fresh or frozen unsweetened blueberries (about 1 quart fresh or 24 ounces frozen)
4 cups water
¼ cup cornstarch

¼ cup cold water
¾ cup sugar
1 cinnamon stick, about 3 inches long
½ cup frozen fat-free or light whipped topping, thawed (optional)

In a large nonaluminum saucepan, combine berries and 4 cups water. Bring to a boil over high heat. Remove from heat. Drain in a sieve; press berries through sieve, returning liquid and pulp to saucepan and discarding any remaining solids.

Meanwhile, put cornstarch in a cup. Add ¼ cup cold water, stirring to dissolve.

Add sugar and cinnamon stick to blueberries. Bring to a boil over high heat; reduce heat to low and whisk in cornstarch mixture. Cook until slightly thickened, about 5 minutes, whisking constantly. Discard cinnamon stick. Chill mixture for at least 2 hours.

To serve, divide kissel among six dessert bowls. Garnish each serving with a dollop of whipped topping.

Calories 171
Protein 1 g
Carbohydrates 44 g
Fiber 3 g
Total Fat 0 g
  Saturated 0 g
  Polyunsaturated 0 g
  Monounsaturated 0 g
Cholesterol 0 mg
Sodium 12 mg

oranges in caramel

SERVES 8; ABOUT 5 ORANGE SLICES AND 2 TABLESPOONS SAUCE PER SERVING

The sweet-bitter caramel perfectly balances the sharp citrus flavor of the oranges in this easy-to-make, refreshing dessert.

6 large navel oranges
4 cups water
1 cup sugar

$\frac{1}{2}$ cup water
$\frac{1}{2}$ cup very hot water

Peel oranges, reserving peel from one orange and discarding remaining peel. Remove any white pith clinging to reserved peel and cut zest into $\frac{1}{4}$-inch-wide strips. In a medium saucepan, bring 4 cups water to a boil over high heat. Blanch orange strips for 5 minutes; drain and set strips aside.

Meanwhile, cut oranges crosswise into $\frac{1}{2}$-inch slices and arrange in overlapping layers in a heatproof serving dish (a $13 \times 9 \times 2$-inch baking dish works well). (Cover with plastic wrap and refrigerate if not using immediately. Recipe can be made up to one day ahead to this point.)

In a small, heavy-bottom saucepan, combine sugar and $\frac{1}{2}$ cup water; stir to wet sugar. Bring to a boil over medium heat without stirring; reduce heat and simmer for 1 minute, or until sugar is completely dissolved. Increase heat to medium-high and boil until syrup is golden or reaches 300°F on a candy thermometer or instant-read thermometer, 5 to 8 minutes, still without stirring. Be careful, because mixture will darken very quickly once it starts to color. Remove from heat and let sit for 30 seconds.

Tilting pan away from you so mixture doesn't splatter, slowly and carefully pour in $\frac{1}{2}$ cup very hot water. Cook over medium heat, stirring constantly, until water is incorporated and any hard caramel has dissolved. Pour caramel over oranges and sprinkle with reserved orange strips. Serve immediately or at room temperature.

CLEMENTINES IN CARAMEL

From November through April, look for clementines, a type of mandarin orange that is small, sweet, and seedless. Substitute 10 sectioned clementines for sliced navel oranges. Use the blanched peel from 3 clementines instead of the blanched orange peel.

COOK'S TIP: For a different, but equally delicious, presentation, refrigerate this dish overnight. The caramel will gradually melt and yield a runny, but tasty, syrup.

Calories 163
Protein 1 g
Carbohydrates 42 g
Fiber 4 g
Total Fat 0 g
  Saturated 0 g
  Polyunsaturated 0 g
  Monounsaturated 0 g
Cholesterol 0 mg
Sodium 1 mg

Sunset Sorbet

Zinfandel Granita

Tropical Bombe

"Watermelon" Bombe

Green Tea and Banana Frozen Yogurt in Crispy Baskets

Espresso Ice Cream Cookie Wrap-Ups

Banana Split Burrito

Baked Apple Parfait

Raspberry Swirl

frozen delights

sunset sorbet

SERVES 6; $1/2$ CUP PER SERVING

Juice from blood oranges gives this sorbet its deep red-orange color, reminiscent of Hawaiian sunsets.

1 cup sugar
1 cup water
1 tablespoon orange-blossom or plain honey

1 tablespoon fresh lemon juice
2 cups blood orange juice (about 6 medium blood oranges)

In a medium saucepan, bring sugar and water to a rapid boil over high heat. Remove from heat.

Whisk in honey and lemon juice. Let sit at room temperature until cool to the touch, about 20 minutes; do not refrigerate.

Stir in orange juice.

Using manufacturer's instructions, freeze sorbet in an ice cream freezer. Immediately place sorbet in freezer for at least 45 minutes to finish firming. If well sealed, sorbet will keep for up to three months in freezer.

COOK'S TIP: Sorbet won't reach the proper consistency in an ice cream freezer. To harden it completely, continue freezing the sorbet in the "real" freezer.

COOK'S TIP ON BLOOD ORANGES: January through March is the season for blood oranges. On the outside, they look like other oranges, but when you cut one open, you'll see how this orange got its less-than-appealing name. Depending on the variety, the flesh is either deep red or whitish with red veins throughout. The juice is a deep red-orange color.

Calories 178
Protein 1 g
Carbohydrates 45 g
Fiber 0 g
Total Fat 0 g
  Saturated 0 g
  Polyunsaturated 0 g
  Monounsaturated 0 g
Cholesterol 0 mg
Sodium 3 mg

zinfandel granita

*This sophisticated version of childhood snowballs is ideal for patio entertaining. There's a bonus:
Because it's made with alcohol, the granita won't freeze solid. That means it will be ready to
enjoy at a moment's notice—perfect for those unexpected adult guests.*

1 $^1/_4$ cups water	$^1/_3$ cup orange juice
$^1/_3$ cup sugar	1 tablespoon lime juice
1 $^1/_2$ cups red zinfandel or any other dry or	
semi-dry red wine (regular or nonalcoholic)	

In a medium saucepan, whisk together water and sugar; bring to a
boil over high heat. Boil for 1 minute, or until sugar dissolves, stirring
constantly. Remove from heat.

Whisk in remaining ingredients. Pour into a $12 \times 8 \times 2$-inch glass
dish; cover with aluminum foil and put in freezer overnight. Chill
wine goblets or individual bowls, if desired.

To serve, run a fork over granita to break it up, then stir to a fluffy
consistency. Spoon into goblets or bowls. Store remaining granita in
an airtight plastic freezer bag for up to two weeks in freezer.

Calories 69
Protein 0 g
Carbohydrates 10 g
Fiber 0 g
Total Fat 0 g
  Saturated 0 g
  Polyunsaturated 0 g
  Monounsaturated 0 g
Cholesterol 0 mg
Sodium 4 mg

tropical bombe

Perfect to serve on a warm summer evening, this striking dessert can be prepared up to a week before serving. Chilling the serving platter is a nice touch.

1 pint mango or papaya sorbet
½ cup sweetened shredded coconut, toasted (see Cook's Tip on Toasting Coconut, page 53)
1 pint pineapple sherbet or peach sorbet
½ pint fresh raspberries, crushed with a fork (about 1 cup)

1 pint raspberry sorbet
¼ cup sweetened shredded coconut, toasted
Sprigs of fresh mint (optional)
Fresh raspberries (optional)

In a medium bowl, let mango sorbet soften at room temperature for about 20 minutes, stirring occasionally.

Stir in ½ cup coconut. Pack into a small (6-cup) ring mold or 9 × 5-inch loaf pan. Press firmly with a rubber scraper and smooth top. Place in freezer for 20 minutes. Meanwhile, let pineapple sherbet soften in a medium bowl.

After the 20 minutes have passed, gently stir raspberries into pineapple sherbet. Spread over mango layer. Return to freezer for 20 minutes. Meanwhile, let raspberry sorbet soften in a medium bowl.

After the 20 minutes have passed, spread raspberry sorbet over pineapple sherbet. Cover with plastic wrap; freeze for at least 4 hours. Chill or freeze serving platter and dessert plates.

Just before serving, partially fill sink with warm tap water. Briefly dip mold or loaf pan in water to within 1 inch of top. Immediately invert onto serving platter. Cut into 12 slices; garnish each slice with coconut, mint, and raspberries. Return any remaining bombe to same mold, cover tightly with plastic wrap, and freeze for up to one month.

COOK'S TIP: To serve 14 to 16, increase raspberry sorbet to 2 pints. Use a fluted 7- to 8-cup decorative mold.

Calories 119
Protein 1 g
Carbohydrates 24 g
Fiber 1 g
Total Fat 3 g
  Saturated 2 g
  Polyunsaturated 0 g
  Monounsaturated 0 g
Cholesterol 2 mg
Sodium 56 mg

"watermelon" bombe

Chocolate "seeds" dot this refreshing, easy-to-make dessert, which looks like half a watermelon. Try it the next time you have a barbecue or a backyard picnic.

1   quart lime sherbet

1   quart raspberry sherbet

3/4   cup miniature chocolate chips

Put serving platter in refrigerator to chill.

Let lime sherbet stand at room temperature for about 10 minutes.

Line a 3-quart metal mixing bowl with plastic wrap, making sure to overlap bowl all around.

For the watermelon "rind," scoop lime sherbet into bowl. Using back of a large metal spoon, spread sherbet evenly over bottom and up sides of bowl all the way to top, completely lining bowl. Place another sheet of plastic wrap on lime sherbet layer; smooth sherbet with your hands. Put bowl in freezer for about 30 minutes while preparing filling.

For the watermelon "flesh," scoop raspberry sherbet into a large mixing bowl; add chocolate chips for "seeds." Using an electric mixer (preferably with a paddle), mix chocolate chips into sherbet until evenly blended. (Sherbet should soften but not melt.)

Remove sherbet-lined bowl from freezer. Remove top layer of plastic wrap. Spoon raspberry mixture into center and press evenly to smooth. Cover with plastic wrap and freeze for at least 2 hours.

Remove from freezer 5 to 10 minutes before serving. Unmold onto chilled serving platter and remove plastic wrap. Using a heavy, straight-edged knife, cut bombe into quarters. Turn pieces upright and slice each quarter into four wedges, just as you would slice a watermelon.

Calories 158
Protein 0 g
Carbohydrates 32 g
Fiber 0 g
Total Fat 3 g
  Saturated 1 g
  Polyunsaturated 0 g
  Monounsaturated 1 g
Cholesterol 3 mg
Sodium 33 mg

green tea and banana frozen yogurt in crispy baskets

Perhaps the most refreshing and exotic way to enjoy green tea on a warm summer day is this unusual Asian-flavored dessert. The crispy baskets are so easy to make with egg roll wrappers. Tea, anyone?

yogurt

$1/2$	cup fat-free milk
2	bags green tea, tags removed
2	medium bananas
$1\,1/2$	cups fat-free or low-fat plain yogurt
$1/4$	cup sugar
2	to 4 drops green food coloring (optional)

baskets

2	egg roll wrappers
	Butter-flavor vegetable oil spray

❖

1	tangelo, tangerine, or orange, peeled if desired (optional)
2	slices crystallized ginger, cut into thin strips (about 1 heaping tablespoon)

For yogurt, in a small microwave-safe bowl, heat milk and tea bags, uncovered, on 100 percent power (high) for 1 minute, or until mixture is hot. Cover and let stand for 5 minutes. Squeeze any excess liquid from tea bags into milk; discard tea bags. Replace cover and refrigerate milk for 15 minutes to 24 hours.

In a medium bowl, mash bananas with a fork. Stir in chilled milk mixture, yogurt, and sugar.

Color mixture with green food coloring. Pour into an 8-inch square nonstick or glass baking dish; cover with plastic wrap. Freeze mixture for 2 to 3 hours (glass may take longer), stirring every hour. (See Cook's Tip, opposite.)

Meanwhile, for baskets, cut each egg roll wrapper into four squares. Lightly spray each side with vegetable oil spray. Spray outside surface of bottom of a 5- or 6-ounce custard cup or ramekin with vegetable oil spray; place sprayed side up on a small microwave-safe plate. Drape one egg roll square over custard cup, letting sides of dough hang over cup. Microwave on 100 percent power (high) for 1 minute, or until edges are slightly brown; be careful not to let edges burn. Gently remove basket from cup; place on a cooling rack. Repeat with remaining wrappers (you can reuse cup without respraying). You will have two extra baskets, which you can use to hold a sundae or eat as a snack.

Calories 142
Protein 5 g
Carbohydrates 30 g
Fiber 1 g
Total Fat 1 g
  Saturated 0 g
  Polyunsaturated 0 g
  Monounsaturated 0 g
Cholesterol 2 mg
Sodium 104 mg

To serve, cut tangelo into 6 wedges. Place each basket on a small plate. Put a ½-cup scoop of frozen yogurt in each basket. Garnish with a wedge of tangelo and a sprinkling of ginger.

COOK'S TIP: You can use the yogurt right away or freeze it for up to one month. If you do so, the yogurt will become very firm. Let it stand at room temperature for 3 to 5 minutes to soften. If you prefer, freeze the yogurt in ice cube trays and process the cubes in a food processor for 1 minute, or until you can scoop the yogurt with an ice-cream scoop.

COOK'S TIP ON EGG ROLL WRAPPERS: Look for packages of egg roll wrappers in the produce section of most grocery stores or Asian markets. You can freeze leftover wrappers for up to six months in an airtight container.

espresso ice cream cookie wrap-ups

Ice cream cookies that please the big kids too! The rich taste of coffee comes through in every morsel. Think you don't like coffee? These treats will change your mind.

1   tablespoon plus 1 1/2 teaspoons instant coffee granules
1   tablespoon hot tap water

16 reduced-fat thin chocolate wafer cookies
1   cup nonfat vanilla ice cream or frozen yogurt

Tear off eight 8 × 12-inch sheets of aluminum foil.

In a cup, stir together coffee granules and water until granules have completely dissolved.

To assemble, put one cookie on center of each sheet of foil; top each cookie with 2 tablespoons ice cream. Working quickly, use a fork to slightly flatten ice cream. Spoon 1/2 teaspoon coffee mixture over each serving. Lightly press remaining cookies on ice cream, allowing coffee to drip slightly. Fold long sides of foil so they overlap at center; twist ends so packet resembles a piece of wrapped candy. Place in freezer for 1 hour to one week before serving in wrappers.

Calories 60
Protein 1 g
Carbohydrates 12 g
Fiber 0 g
Total Fat 1g
  Saturated 0 g
  Polyunsaturated 0 g
  Monounsaturated 0 g
Cholesterol 0 mg
Sodium 59 mg

banana split burrito

A classic gets a Tex-Mex twist with all the trimmings. Serve it after your next Southwestern meal.

Vegetable oil spray
2 teaspoons sugar
1/8 teaspoon ground cinnamon
2 6-inch nonfat or reduced-fat flour tortillas
  Butter-flavor vegetable oil spray
2 medium bananas
1/4 cup fat-free hot fudge sauce
2 cups fat-free or light vanilla frozen yogurt

1 cup fresh hulled and sliced strawberries (about 1/2 pint)
1/2 cup drained canned pineapple tidbits in their own juice
1/2 cup frozen fat-free or light whipped topping, thawed
1 tablespoon plus 1 teaspoon chopped pecans
4 maraschino cherries

Preheat oven to 450°F. Spray a baking sheet with vegetable oil spray. Set aside.

In a small bowl, stir together sugar and cinnamon.

Place 1 tortilla on a microwave-safe plate. Cook, uncovered, on 100 percent power (high) for 5 to 15 seconds, or until warm and softened.

Lightly spray both sides of tortilla with vegetable oil spray. Sprinkle both sides with sugar mixture. Place banana in center of tortilla; roll tortilla jelly-roll style and secure in two places with wooden toothpicks. Cut tortilla in half crosswise and place on baking sheet. Repeat with remaining tortilla and banana.

Bake, uncovered, for 8 to 10 minutes, or until tortillas are crisp and slightly golden brown.

Meanwhile, in a small saucepan, warm hot fudge sauce over low heat.

To assemble, place a banana burrito in each of four bowls. Top each with 1/2 cup frozen yogurt, 1/4 cup strawberries, 2 tablespoons pineapple, 1 tablespoon hot fudge sauce, 2 tablespoons whipped topping, 1 teaspoon chopped pecans, and a cherry, or arrange around burrito.

Calories 316
Protein 8 g
Carbohydrates 69 g
Fiber 4 g
Total Fat 2 g
  Saturated 0 g
  Polyunsaturated 1 g
  Monounsaturated 1 g
Cholesterol 2 mg
Sodium 249 mg

baked apple parfait

Sweet bits of apple create their own sauce while they cook, then are tossed with dry-roasted nuts and served piping hot over ice cream. Pure delight!

8 ounces Red Delicious apple, peeled and cut into 1/2-inch cubes

2 teaspoons sugar

1/4 teaspoon ground cinnamon

1 1/2 teaspoons chilled acceptable stick margarine (not light margarine)

2 tablespoons nut topping

1/4 teaspoon vanilla, butter, and nut flavoring or vanilla extract

1 pint fat-free or reduced-fat vanilla ice cream (2 cups)

2 tablespoons plus 2 teaspoons fat-free caramel topping

Preheat oven to 350°F. Put four individual serving dishes in freezer, if desired.

Put apples in an 8-inch square nonstick baking pan.

In a small bowl, stir together sugar and cinnamon. Sprinkle over apples.

Dot apples with margarine. Cover pan tightly with aluminum foil.

Bake for 15 minutes (longer if you like apples softer).

Meanwhile, put nut topping on a sheet of aluminum foil. When apples have baked for 15 minutes, place nut topping on oven rack beside apples. Bake for 5 minutes, or until apples are crisp-tender and nuts are fragrant.

Stir nut topping and vanilla, butter, and nut flavoring into apples.

To assemble, scoop 1/2 cup ice cream into each dessert dish, drizzle 2 teaspoons caramel sauce over each serving, and spoon about 1/4 cup apple mixture over each. Serve immediately.

COOK'S TIP ON NUT TOPPING: Nut topping is usually found in the supermarket near the nuts. It contains fewer fat grams per serving than plain nuts.

Calories 214
Protein 5 g
Carbohydrates 43 g
Fiber 1 g
Total Fat 3 g
  Saturated 1 g
  Polyunsaturated — g
  Monounsaturated — g
Cholesterol 0 mg
Sodium 131 mg

raspberry swirl

Delicious and light, this frosty dessert is a sure palate-pleaser.

crust

3/4 cup reduced-fat graham cracker crumbs (about 12 squares)

3 tablespoons fat-free tub margarine, melted

1 tablespoon plus 1½ teaspoons sugar

filling

1 10- to 12-ounce package frozen lightly sweetened raspberries or unsweetened blackberries, thawed

1 8-ounce package fat-free cream cheese, room temperature

1 cup sugar

2 cups frozen fat-free or light whipped topping, thawed (about 5 ounces)

For crust, in a small bowl, combine ingredients. Press mixture onto bottom of a 9-inch square glass baking dish. Set aside.

For filling, in a food processor or blender, puree raspberries. Set aside.

In a medium mixing bowl, beat cream cheese with an electric mixer on low until light and fluffy.

Add 1 cup sugar and beat until well blended.

Fold whipped topping into cream cheese mixture.

Fold in raspberries. Spread mixture over crust.

Cover with plastic wrap and freeze for at least 2 hours, or until firm. Cut into 16 squares and serve immediately.

COOK'S TIP: If you can't find frozen raspberries that aren't packed in syrup, reduce the amount of sugar in the filling to ¼ cup.

Calories 115
Protein 3 g
Carbohydrates 25 g
Fiber 1 g
Total Fat 0 g
  Saturated 0 g
  Polyunsaturated 0 g
  Monounsaturated 0 g
Cholesterol 1 mg
Sodium 112 mg

Spanish Wind Cake

Pear Spring Rolls with Citrus Dipping Sauce

Crispy Strawberry Napoleons

Apricot Lunch Box Treats

Baked Sopaipillas

Filled Dessert Rolls

Pecan Brittle Crunch

Butter Toffee Syrup

Fudge-Mint Syrup

Raspberry Sauce

Mocha Coffee Sauce

Mocha Frosting

other
temp-
tations

spanish wind cake

The smooth surface of this truly spectacular dessert is reminiscent of the wind that blows in Spain in the spring. You can make the meringue shell far in advance. Don't be daunted by the length of the instructions—this show-stopping dessert really isn't difficult to make. By changing the filling, you can create almost endless variations.

basket

Whites of 5 large eggs, room temperature
1/4 teaspoon salt
1 teaspoon vinegar
1 1/3 cups sugar
1 tablespoon plus 1 1/2 teaspoons cornstarch
1/2 teaspoon vanilla extract
1/4 teaspoon almond extract

mortar

Whites of 5 large eggs, room temperature
1/4 teaspoon salt
1 teaspoon vinegar
1 1/4 cups sugar
1 tablespoon plus 1 1/2 teaspoons cornstarch
1/2 teaspoon vanilla extract
1/4 teaspoon almond extract

filling

1 pint lemon ice milk
1 pint strawberry ice milk
2 cups fresh strawberries, blueberries, blackberries, or raspberries, or a combination (about 1 pint)

Preheat oven to 250°F. Line two large baking sheets with cooking parchment, then draw one 7-inch circle and four 8-inch circles on parchment with a dark thin marker. Flip parchment over (drawn lines will show through). Set aside.

Make meringue in two batches, one for basket, or structure of the cake, one for "mortar." For the basket, in a large mixing bowl, beat egg whites with an electric mixer on high until soft peaks form.

Beat in salt and vinegar.

In a small bowl, stir together sugar and cornstarch. Add sugar mixture, 1 to 2 tablespoons at a time, to egg whites, beating after each addition until meringue is very stiff and glossy. (Peaks shouldn't fold over when beater is lifted, and meringue shouldn't feel gritty when rubbed between fingers.)

Beat in extracts.

Using a pastry bag without a tip, outline all five circles with meringue. Solidly fill in 7-inch circle and one 8-inch circle (8-inch circle will become bottom of cake and 7-inch circle will be lid). For remaining three circles, pipe a row of meringue on top of existing row to make 1-inch-high rings (rings will be stacked on the 8-inch circle to form sides of basket).

Calories 190
Protein 4 g
Carbohydrates 42 g
Fiber 0 g
Total Fat 2 g
  Saturated 1 g
  Polyunsaturated 0 g
  Monounsaturated 0 g
Cholesterol 5 mg
Sodium 136 mg

Bake for 45 minutes, or until cream colored. Leave oven on. Transfer meringues, still on cooking parchment, to cooling racks. Loosen meringues from parchment and allow to cool on parchment.

Meanwhile, make second batch of meringue, the "mortar," using instructions above (you don't need baking sheets or parchment for this batch).

To form basket, frost top of baked 8-inch solid base with unbaked meringue. Using unbaked meringue between layers to seal them together, stack each ring on base. Frost outside of basket with meringue. Frost the solid top with meringue. Using a pastry bag and a large star tip, decorate lid and, if desired, basket with remaining meringue. (If meringue doesn't hold a distinct shape as it comes out of tip, wipe tip with a damp cloth.)

Bake basket and top for 1 hour. Transfer meringues, still on cooking parchment, to cooling rack and let cool completely, about 30 minutes. If not planning to assemble basket immediately, turn off oven and allow meringues to cool on baking sheet in oven.

Fill shell with scoops of ice milk and berries. Top with lid. Keep frozen until needed. To serve, cut into wedges, then lift onto plates with a cake server and a spoon.

COOK'S TIP: You'll need a cotton or paper pastry bag for pressing out the meringue. (Plastic will cause the meringue to break down and become sticky.)

You can store the basket in an airtight container in a dry place or fill it immediately, wrap it well, and freeze it until ready to serve. The frozen cake is easy to serve if you use a fork to cut through to make wedges rather than using a knife to cut down, which compresses the meringue and makes it tough. An angel food cutter is ideal, but dinner forks work well too.

pear spring rolls with citrus dipping sauce

SERVES 4; 1 SPRING ROLL, 2 TABLESPOONS YOGURT, AND $1/4$ CUP MANDARIN ORANGES PER SERVING

When you want a dessert that is not too filling after a hearty, heart-healthful meal, this artfully arranged Asian-flavored sensation provides the finishing touch. You can also pack the spring rolls—with or without the sauce—for something different in your brown bag.

Butter-flavor vegetable oil spray
2 medium pears, such as Anjou, Bartlett, or Bosc (10 to 12 ounces)
$1/4$ cup golden raisins
2 tablespoons chopped walnuts
1 tablespoon light brown sugar
1 teaspoon chopped crystallized ginger (about 1 slice) or $1/8$ teaspoon ground ginger
1 teaspoon cornstarch
1 teaspoon lemon juice
$1/8$ cup mandarin oranges, canned in water or light syrup, drained and finely chopped (optional)

$1/8$ teaspoon ground mace or ground nutmeg
8 sheets (about 12 x $16^1/2$ inches) frozen phyllo dough, thawed
Butter-flavor vegetable oil spray
1 11-ounce can mandarin oranges in water or light syrup, drained
$1/2$ cup fat-free or low-fat flavored yogurt, such as mandarin orange, tangerine, vanilla, peach, apricot, apricot mango, or raspberry
Ground mace or ground nutmeg (optional)

Preheat oven to 375°F. Spray a rimmed baking sheet with vegetable oil spray.

Peel pears and chop into $1/4$- to $1/2$-inch cubes. In a large bowl, combine pears, raisins, walnuts, brown sugar, ginger, cornstarch, lemon juice, and $1/8$ teaspoon mace.

Keeping unused phyllo covered with a damp dish towel or damp paper towels to prevent drying, lightly spray one side of a sheet of dough with vegetable oil spray. Place short end toward you. Lay another sheet on the first and lightly spray with vegetable oil spray. Spoon about $1/3$ cup pear mixture in center, spreading it so you leave about a 2-inch border all around dough. Fold about 2 inches of each long side toward center of dough. Starting at one short end, roll dough jelly-roll style to enclose filling (you'll have a cylinder shaped like a spring roll). Lightly spray with vegetable oil spray; place seam side down on baking sheet. Repeat with remaining phyllo dough and pear mixture.

Bake for 18 to 20 minutes, or until dough is light golden brown. Remove from baking sheet and let cool on a cooling rack for 5 to 10 minutes.

Calories 290
Protein 6 g
Carbohydrates 58 g
Fiber 4 g
Total Fat 5 g
  Saturated 1 g
  Polyunsaturated 2 g
  Monounsaturated 2 g
Cholesterol 1 mg
Sodium 211 mg

To serve, decoratively arrange ¼ cup mandarin oranges on each of four plates. Cut each warm spring roll in half diagonally; place two halves of spring roll on each plate. Spoon 2 tablespoons yogurt and 1½ teaspoons mandarin oranges into each of four small bowls for dipping; sprinkle yogurt with mace.

COOK'S TIP: For a more exotic taste, combine the yogurt with 1 tablespoon honey, ½ teaspoon grated lemon, tangerine, orange, grapefruit, lime, or tangelo zest, and ¼ teaspoon poppy seeds. If you wish, save about ¼ cup of the drained mandarin oranges, coarsely chop them, and add them to the dipping sauce.

crispy strawberry napoleons

Phyllo dough provides a terrific low-fat alternative to puff pastry dough in these vibrant napoleons.

¼ cup sugar
1 teaspoon ground cinnamon
3 sheets (about 12 x 16½ inches) frozen phyllo dough, thawed
   Butter-flavor vegetable oil spray
1 pint fresh strawberries, hulled and sliced (about 2 cups)

2 tablespoons confectioners' sugar
2 cups frozen fat-free or light whipped topping, thawed (about 5 ounces)
   Sifted confectioners' sugar (optional)

Preheat oven to 375°F.

In a small bowl, stir together sugar and cinnamon.

Cover phyllo with a damp dish towel or damp paper towels. Working quickly, lay 1 sheet of phyllo on a large sheet of cooking parchment; spray phyllo lightly but evenly with vegetable oil spray. Sprinkle with 1 tablespoon sugar mixture. Spray both sides of another sheet of phyllo, then stack it directly over first sheet; sprinkle with 1 table-spoon sugar mixture. Repeat with remaining phyllo; sprinkle with remaining sugar mixture. Using kitchen scissors, cut parchment and phyllo stack in half crosswise, forming two 12 × 8¼-inch rectangles. Transfer phyllo stacks, still on cooking parchment, to two baking sheets.

Bake for 10 to 12 minutes, or until phyllo is golden brown and crisp. Using a long, sharp knife, preferably a chef's knife, cut each cooled phyllo rectangle into six rectangles, 4 × 2¾ inches each. (To get this size, cut each rectangle into thirds crosswise and lengthwise.) Let cool completely on cooling racks.

Meanwhile, in a medium bowl, combine strawberries and confection-ers' sugar.

To assemble, for each serving, arrange one phyllo rectangle on a serv-ing plate and top with ¼ cup whipped topping and ¼ cup berries; repeat, then top with a third phyllo rectangle. Dust with confection-ers' sugar.

Calories 128
Protein 1 g
Carbohydrates 28 g
Fiber 2 g
Total Fat 1 g
  Saturated 0 g
  Polyunsaturated 0 g
  Monounsaturated 0 g
Cholesterol 0 mg
Sodium 60 mg

apricot lunch box treats

Under each plump apricot half, melted marshmallows sit on a gingersnap crust. The kids will love these unusual sweets, especially if you make them together.

3/4 cup coarse gingersnap cookie crumbs (about 12 cookies)

1 tablespoon plus 2 teaspoons orange juice

1 teaspoon light corn syrup

1/4 cup plus 2 tablespoons miniature marshmallows, plain or fruit flavor (about 48)

1 15-ounce can apricot halves in extra-light syrup, drained
Butter-flavor vegetable oil spray

1 tablespoon light brown sugar

1/8 to 1/4 teaspoon ground cinnamon

Preheat oven to 350°F. Place foil or paper liners in six 2¾-inch muffin cups.

Pour crumbs into a small bowl; stir in orange juice and corn syrup. Spoon about 2 tablespoons mixture into each liner. Place a piece of plastic wrap over each liner and press down mixture to cover bottom of liner (plastic wrap prevents mixture from sticking to your fingers); remove plastic wrap.

Bake for 10 minutes. Remove muffin tin from oven, but leave oven on.

To assemble, spoon 1 tablespoon marshmallows over one crust. Place an apricot half cut side down over marshmallows. Lightly spray top of apricot with vegetable oil spray. Sprinkle with ½ teaspoon brown sugar and a dash of cinnamon. Repeat with remaining ingredients.

Bake for 8 to 10 minutes, or until brown sugar has dissolved and marshmallows are melted and oozing from sides of apricots. Remove from muffin tin and let cool for 5 minutes. Serve warm or chilled.

Calories 99
Protein 1 g
Carbohydrates 21 g
Fiber 1 g
Total Fat 1 g
  Saturated 0 g
  Polyunsaturated 0 g
  Monounsaturated 1 g
Cholesterol 0 mg
Sodium 96 mg

baked sopaipillas

SERVES 8; 4 PER SERVING

After the dough thaws, let your family help you transform it into sopaipillas (so-puh-PEA-yuhz).

Butter-flavor vegetable oil spray
8 raw frozen dinner rolls
2 tablespoons sugar

$1/2$ teaspoon ground cinnamon
$1/3$ cup honey

Lightly spray two large baking sheets with vegetable oil spray. Put rolls about 3 inches apart on one baking sheet; set second baking sheet aside. Lightly spray tops of rolls and a large sheet of plastic wrap with vegetable oil spray. Cover dough lightly with plastic wrap. Using package directions, let dough thaw until soft, about 2 hours (or use package directions for quick-thaw method).

In a small, shallow bowl, combine sugar and cinnamon.

Put a softened roll on a cutting board. Using your hands, stretch dough to a 4-inch circle. Using a pizza cutter or knife, cut circle into quarters. Coat each side of dough pieces with sugar mixture. Put pieces 1 inch apart on reserved baking sheet. Repeat with remaining rolls. Cover dough lightly with plastic wrap and let rise for 1 hour, or until doubled in bulk.

Preheat oven to 350°F.

Bake rolls for 12 to 14 minutes, or until golden brown.

To serve, place four sopaipillas on a dessert plate and drizzle with 2 teaspoons honey. Repeat with remaining pieces and honey.

COOK'S TIP: Sopaipillas will keep in an airtight container for up to three days in the refrigerator. To reheat, put six to eight sopaipillas on a microwave-safe plate. Heat, uncovered, on 100 percent power (high) for 30 to 45 seconds, or until warmed through.

Calories 159
Protein 4g
Carbohydrates 33 g
Fiber 1 g
Total Fat 2 g
  Saturated 0 g
  Polyunsaturated — g
  Monounsaturated — g
Cholesterol 0 mg
Sodium 149 mg

filled dessert rolls

Rolls for dessert? When they resemble jelly-filled doughnuts, give them a try! Let frozen dough thaw while you work or sleep, then pop the rolls into the oven for dessert or breakfast.

Butter-flavored vegetable oil spray
8 raw frozen dinner rolls
2 tablespoons sugar
1/2 teaspoon ground cinnamon

1/2 to 1 cup light pie filling, all-fruit spread, or pudding made with fat-free milk, any flavor
1/2 cup sifted confectioners' sugar

Lightly spray a large baking sheet with vegetable oil spray. Put rolls about 3 inches apart on baking sheet. Lightly spray tops with vegetable oil spray. Cover lightly with plastic wrap. Using package directions, let dough thaw until rolls have doubled in size. (This usually takes 4 to 6 hours; some directions include a quick-thaw method. For rolls with a very light texture, let dough thaw for 7 to 8 hours.)

Preheat oven to 350°F.

In a small bowl, stir together sugar and cinnamon. Sprinkle over rolls.

Bake for 18 to 20 minutes, or until rolls are golden brown. Put baking sheet on cooling rack and let rolls cool for 10 minutes.

Using handle of a wooden spoon or other thin, round object, poke a hole in side of each roll without going through other side. Rotate handle inside roll to create a space for filling. Use a small spoon, such as a 1/4-teaspoon measuring spoon, or pastry bag to fill each roll with your choice of filling.

Put confectioners' sugar in a shallow bowl. Add one roll at a time, turning to coat evenly. Shake off excess sugar.

COOK'S TIP: Filled rolls keep in an airtight container in the refrigerator for up to three days. but it's a good idea to wait until serving time to coat them with confectioners' sugar.

Calories 167
Protein 4 g
Carbohydrates 34 g
Fiber 1 g
Total Fat 3 g
 Saturated 0 g
 Polyunsaturated 0 g
 Monounsaturated 0 g
Cholesterol 0 mg
Sodium 152 mg

pecan brittle crunch

This crunchy, buttery, nutty topping brings out the kid in everyone. Sprinkle it over fat-free ice cream or baked fruit, such as apples, peaches, or bananas, or serve larger pieces as a candy treat.

Butter-flavor vegetable oil spray
1 tablespoon acceptable stick margarine
2/3 cup sugar

1/4 teaspoon salt
2 tablespoons finely chopped pecans

Spray one side of a 12-inch piece of aluminum foil with vegetable oil spray. Set aside.

Spray a large nonstick skillet with vegetable oil spray; heat over medium heat until hot. Melt margarine and swirl to coat bottom of skillet.

Stir in sugar and salt; cook for 10 minutes, stirring occasionally.

Stir in pecans; cook for 5 minutes, stirring frequently. Cook for 2 minutes, stirring constantly. Pour onto foil; using back of spoon, quickly spread evenly in a thin layer. Let cool completely, 12 to 15 minutes.

Fold edges of aluminum foil over hardened mixture to cover completely. Using back of a spoon, tap foil to crumble mixture into fairly coarse pieces. Store for up to three days in an airtight container in a cool, dry place, such as a pantry or kitchen cupboard.

Calories 119
Protein 0 g
Carbohydrates 23 g
Fiber 0 g
Total Fat 4 g
  Saturated 1 g
  Polyunsaturated 1 g
  Monounsaturated 2 g
Cholesterol 0 mg
Sodium 119 mg

butter toffee syrup

SERVES 4; 2 TABLESPOONS PER SERVING

*This thick, gooey syrup has all the flavor of old-fashioned butterscotch candies.
Try it over fat-free ice cream or raw, baked, or poached fruit.*

¼ cup firmly packed dark brown sugar
¼ cup light corn syrup
2 tablespoons fat-free milk
⅛ teaspoon salt

1 tablespoon acceptable stick margarine
½ teaspoon vanilla, butter, and nut flavoring
  or vanilla extract

In a small saucepan, whisk together brown sugar, corn syrup, milk, and salt. Bring to a boil over medium heat; boil for 1 minute, whisking constantly. Remove from heat.

Whisk in remaining ingredients. Let cool completely to thicken, 20 to 25 minutes. Serve warm or cold. Syrup can be refrigerated for up to two weeks in a jar with a tight-fitting lid.

FUDGE-MINT SYRUP

Add 3 tablespoons unsweetened cocoa powder to corn syrup mixture before cooking. Substitute peppermint extract for vanilla, butter, and nut flavoring. Serves 5; 2 tablespoons per serving.

BUTTER TOFFEE SYRUP	
Calories	139
Protein	0 g
Carbohydrates	30 g
Fiber	0 g
Total Fat	3 g
Saturated	1 g
Polyunsaturated	1 g
Monounsaturated	1 g
Cholesterol	0 mg
Sodium	140 mg

FUDGE-MINT SYRUP	
Calories	119
Protein	1 g
Carbohydrates	25 g
Fiber	1 g
Total Fat	3 g
Saturated	1 g
Polyunsaturated	1 g
Monounsaturated	1 g
Cholesterol	0 mg
Sodium	113 mg

raspberry sauce

*The intense flavor in this sauce comes from a double dose of raspberries.
The sauce is wonderful drizzled over vanilla or chocolate pudding,
vanilla Bavarian cream, raspberry sherbet, or vanilla ice milk.*

20 ounces frozen raspberries in syrup, thawed (about 2 cups)
1/4 cup water
2 tablespoons raspberry-flavored liqueur

1 tablespoon light corn syrup
2 teaspoons cornstarch

In a food processor or blender, process raspberries and syrup until smooth. Press puree through a fine sieve into a measuring cup; if necessary, add water so you have 2 cups. Pour into a small saucepan.

Whisk remaining ingredients into puree. Cook over medium heat until thickened and bubbly, about 5 minutes, whisking constantly. Remove from heat and let cool completely, about 30 minutes, at room temperature. Sauce can be refrigerated in a jar with a tight-fitting lid for up to one week.

Calories 96
Protein 1 g
Carbohydrates 23 g
Fiber 3 g
Total Fat 0 g
 Saturated 0 g
 Polyunsaturated 0 g
 Monounsaturated 0 g
Cholesterol 0 mg
Sodium 4 mg

pear spring rolls with citrus dipping sauce *(page 148)*

lime fool with raspberries and kiwifruit *(page 105)*

sweet-spiced fruit with cabernet sauce *(page 121)*

triple-berry, triple-citrus summer pudding
(page 114)

tropical bombe *(page 136)*

double-chocolate valentine cake *(page 82)*

"watermelon" bombe *(page 137)*

banana split burrito *(page 141)*

crispy strawberry napoleons *(page 150)*

spanish wind cake *(page 146)*

mocha coffee sauce

SERVES 12; ABOUT 2 TABLESPOONS PER SERVING

Coffee-flavored liqueur enhances this irresistible sauce. Try it drizzled over vanilla ice milk or as a topping for angel food cake with a scoop of strawberry ice milk.

²/₃ cup sugar

²/₃ cup unsweetened cocoa powder (Dutch process preferred)

²/₃ cup hot coffee, or ²/₃ cup hot water and 1 tablespoon instant coffee granules

¹/₃ cup light corn syrup

3 tablespoons coffee-flavored liqueur

1 teaspoon vanilla extract

Calories 103
Protein 1 g
Carbohydrates 23 g
Fiber 1 g
Total Fat 0 g
Saturated 0 g
Polyunsaturated 0 g
Monounsaturated 0 g
Cholesterol 0 mg
Sodium 14 mg

In a medium saucepan, whisk together sugar, cocoa powder, coffee, and corn syrup. Bring to a boil over medium heat, whisking frequently.

Add liqueur and boil for 1 minute, whisking constantly. Remove from heat and let cool for about 30 minutes.

Stir in vanilla. Cover and refrigerate for 1 to 2 hours. Sauce can be refrigerated in a jar with a tight-fitting lid for up to one week.

mocha frosting

SERVES 8; 2 TABLESPOONS PER SERVING (ENOUGH FOR ONE-LAYER 8- OR 9-INCH CAKE)

Whether you use it to frost a cake, such as Apple Cappuccino Cake (page 21), or for dipping slices of fresh pears or apples, you'll enjoy this ultra-easy coffee-flavored delight.

1 cup mocha-flavor fat-free liquid nondairy creamer

¹/₂ cup sifted confectioners' sugar

2 tablespoons instant coffee granules

1 tablespoon plus 1 teaspoon cornstarch

1 tablespoon plus 1 teaspoon acceptable vegetable oil

Calories 103
Protein 0 g
Carbohydrates 18 g
Fiber 0 g
Total Fat 2 g
Saturated 0 g
Polyunsaturated 1 g
Monounsaturated 1 g
Cholesterol 0 mg
Sodium 1 mg

In a small saucepan, whisk together all ingredients. Bring to a boil over medium heat, whisking constantly; boil for 30 seconds. Remove from heat. Use immediately, or for a slightly thicker consistency, let cool for about 30 minutes.

fat-free
yogurt

fat-free
Milk

SORBEt

flour

sugar

appendixes

appendix a—heart health

what high blood cholesterol means to your heart

When it comes to eating with your heart in mind, the most important thing you can do is limit the amount and kinds of fat in your diet. That's because certain fats (saturated fat, trans fat, and cholesterol) raise low-density lipoprotein cholesterol (LDL cholesterol), or "bad cholesterol." LDL cholesterol can be deposited in the walls of your arteries as plaque. The buildup of plaque in the blood vessel wall is called atherosclerosis. Atherosclerosis is the process that leads to heart disease and heart attacks.

saturated fat, trans fat, and cholesterol

Saturated fat comes from both animal- and plant-based foods. Animal-based foods high in saturated fat include butter and whole-milk dairy products, organ meats, lard, and beef, pork, and chicken fat. Plant-based foods containing saturated fat include coconut oil, palm kernel oil, palm oil, and cocoa butter.

Trans fats are created when vegetable oil is hydrogenated (hydrogen is added) to make it solid. Some of the most significant sources of trans fats are some kinds of stick margarine and commercially baked products such as cookies, crackers, and breads. Check ingredient labels so you can avoid hydrogenated or partially hydrogenated oils, and select liquid or tub margarine when possible. (The more liquid the form of the margarine, the less trans fat it contains.)

Cholesterol in foods comes exclusively from animal products. It's in all meats, poultry, seafood, and animal fats, such as butter and lard. The richest sources are egg yolks, shellfish, and organ meats.

polyunsaturated and monounsaturated fats

With this information in mind, if you're going to cook with fat, choose the polyunsaturated and monounsaturated varieties. They don't raise LDL cholesterol, the "bad cholesterol." They help increase high-density lipoproteins (HDLs), or the "good cholesterol." In fact, HDL cholesterol can help protect you against having high blood cholesterol and the resulting heart disease that can lead to heart attack.

You'll find polyunsaturated fats in vegetable oils, such as safflower, sunflower, soybean, and corn. You'll also find it in some fish and fish oils. Monounsaturated fat is mostly in olive oil, canola (rapeseed) oil, and some forms of sunflower and safflower oil.

Even though polyunsaturated and monounsaturated fats tend to protect you against heart disease, the important thing when planning your meals—including desserts—is to look at your *total fat and saturated fat intake*. Over a week's time, make sure that no more than 30 percent of your total calories come from fat. No more than 10 percent should come from saturated fat, no more than 10 percent from polyunsaturated fat, and no more than 15 percent from monounsaturated fat. As for cholesterol, keep it to less than 300 milligrams per day. If you have had a heart attack or have coronary heart disease, further restrict your saturated fat intake to less than 7 percent of your total calories per week and your cholesterol intake to less than 200 milligrams per day. Limiting the amount and kinds of fat you eat is a major key to keeping your total blood cholesterol level—along with your risk of heart disease—low.

your blood cholesterol level

Too much cholesterol in the blood is a major risk factor for heart attack, so what *is* a safe blood cholesterol range? Basically, if your total blood cholesterol is less than 200 milligrams per deciliter (mg/dL), you're right where you need to be.

If your total blood cholesterol is between 200 and 239 mg/dL, you have a borderline high-risk cholesterol level. You need to take some steps to reduce it. Total blood cholesterol of 240 mg/dL or higher is high-risk blood cholesterol, and you definitely need to reduce that level. You need to eat less saturated fat and cholesterol and maintain a healthy weight. The best way to do that is to reduce the number of calories you eat and increase your level of physical activity. Work with your doctor to develop a program that is right for you.

"Yikes!" you say. "With all this need to limit fat and calories, I'll bet I can never eat dessert again." Actually you *can* eat dessert—the trick is to balance your food intake for the entire week and choose a dessert that fits in with your plan for good health. That's where this book helps. The desserts on these pages keep saturated fats, cholesterol, and calories—but not flavor—trimmed. Most of the fats in these recipes are polyunsaturated and monounsaturated. You'll also notice that we keep calories to a minimum. Watching calories is key, since maintaining a healthful weight is important to heart health. The American Heart Association has declared obesity as a major risk factor for heart disease (see page 164). Obesity also increases your risk of developing diabetes, another major risk factor for heart disease (see page 165).

By using these recipes and thinking ahead, you can enjoy dessert after some meals, knowing that your planning has let you keep your saturated fat, cholesterol, and calorie intake in the heart-healthy range.

what's *your* risk of heart disease?

Lots of factors influence the risk of getting heart disease. Unfortunately, some of them are things you can't control. On the other hand, most of the risk factors are things you *can* do something about.

risk factors you can't control

AGE
Being 45 years or older for men or 55 years or older for women is one risk factor you can't control.

FAMILY HISTORY OF EARLY HEART DISEASE (HEART ATTACK OR SUDDEN DEATH)
If your father or brother was stricken before age 55 or if your mother or sister was stricken before age 65, that is a risk factor.

BEING MALE
Until about age 65, men are at greater risk of getting heart disease than women. Everyone's blood cholesterol starts rising at about age 20. However, until menopause, women have lower LDL-cholesterol levels than men of the same age. After menopause, a woman's LDL-cholesterol level rises, along with her risk of heart disease.

HEREDITY
Your body actually manufactures all the cholesterol you need. Your genes uniquely influence how your body makes and handles this cholesterol. That's why some people can eat more saturated fat and cholesterol than others without having high blood cholesterol. It's also why some people have high blood cholesterol when they don't eat a lot of fat. A tendency toward heart disease seems to be hereditary too. Race is another consideration.

African-Americans have a greater risk of heart disease and stroke than white Americans.

risk factors you can control

CIGARETTE SMOKING

If you smoke, you have twice the risk of heart attack and two to four times the risk of sudden cardiac death as people who don't smoke. In fact, your risk of death due to heart disease is significantly greater if you're simply exposed to secondhand smoke than if you aren't. The good news is that if you quit smoking, your risk of heart disease immediately begins to decline.

HIGH BLOOD CHOLESTEROL
(HIGH TOTAL CHOLESTEROL AND HIGH LDL CHOLESTEROL)

You can get high blood cholesterol in two main ways. One is from the saturated fat and cholesterol in the foods you eat. Watching your diet is, of course, the way to control the amount of saturated fat and cholesterol you consume. The second way to get high blood cholesterol is from cholesterol that's manufactured naturally in your body. A person's liver can manufacture too much cholesterol. Too much cholesterol in your blood is called hypercholesterolemia, and it may need to be treated with cholesterol-lowering medications, as well as diet, exercise, and weight management.

LOW HDL CHOLESTEROL

Remember that a high HDL-cholesterol level helps protect you against heart disease by removing cholesterol from your bloodstream. If your HDL-cholesterol level is low, talk to your doctor to learn ways to change that. Get 30 to 60 minutes of physical activity three to four days each week, and keep your weight under control.

HIGH BLOOD PRESSURE

Any blood pressure of 140/90 or greater should be treated by a doctor. Fortunately, many effective ways to reduce your blood pressure exist. They include losing weight, exercising, limiting your daily sodium intake to less than 2,400 milligrams, eating at least five servings of fruits and vegetables plus two to four servings of fat-free or low-fat dairy products each day, and if necessary, taking medication.

PHYSICAL INACTIVITY

Exercising regularly—in fact, being active in any way—helps lower your LDL-cholesterol level and raise your HDL-cholesterol level. Getting 30 to 60 minutes of aerobic exercise three or four times a week should go a long way toward keeping your cardiovascular system healthy. Even moderate activity, such as walking for pleasure, gardening, doing housework, and dancing, can have a protective effect.

OBESITY/OVERWEIGHT

Watching calories is very important because obesity by itself is a major risk factor for heart disease. Being overweight can make your LDL-cholesterol level rise and your HDL-cholesterol level fall. Obesity also raises blood pressure and increases your risk of developing diabetes. As a general rule, you are considered obese when your body mass index (BMI) is 30.0 or above. A BMI of 25.0 to 29.9 is considered overweight (see chart below).

body mass index

HEIGHT	OVERWEIGHT (BMI 25.0–29.9)	OBESE (BMI 30.0 AND ABOVE)
4'10"	119–142 lb	143 lb or more
4'11"	124–147	148
5'0"	128–152	153
5'1"	132–157	158
5'2"	136–163	164
5'3"	141–168	169
5'4"	145–173	174
5'5"	150–179	180
5'6"	155–185	186
5'7"	159–190	191
5'8"	164–196	197
5'9"	169–202	203
5'10"	174–208	209
5'11"	179–214	215
6'0"	184–220	221
6'1"	189–226	227
6'2"	194–232	233
6'3"	200–239	240
6'4"	205–245	246

appendix a

DIABETES

Diabetes mellitus is a malfunction in the body's ability to metabolize sugar. In some cases, diabetes can be controlled by diet, weight management, and exercise. In other cases, medication is necessary. If you have diabetes, see your doctor for a treatment plan to keep it under control. A diabetes educator or dietitian can help you plan a healthful way of eating that may also limit the total amount of carbohydrates you consume at each meal.

how to eat as if your heart depends on it: the american heart association diet

At the American Heart Association, we believe that all Americans over the age of two can benefit from following five simple dietary recommendations. (Children under two need more calories from fat.)

1. Eat a wide variety of foods, with plenty of vegetables, fruits, and whole grains to get a balance of nutrients.

2. Balance your food intake with physical activity to achieve and maintain a healthy weight.

3. Choose a diet low in saturated fat, trans fat, and cholesterol and moderate in total fat.

4. Use salt (sodium) and sugar in moderation.

5. If you drink alcohol, do so in moderation.

These few recommendations—a simple way to eat healthfully—are designed to help you eat with your heart in mind. They help reduce your blood cholesterol or prevent high blood cholesterol and prevent or control high blood pressure. Using these guidelines and referring to the chart on page 166 should make it easy as pie to follow the more specific recommendations listed below.

Our recommendations are to eat

❖ less than 10 percent of the week's total calories from saturated fat

❖ 30 percent or less of the week's total calories from fat

❖ less than 300 milligrams of dietary cholesterol a day

❖ just enough calories to achieve and maintain a healthy weight. (Check with your doctor or a registered dietitian for the calorie level that's best for you.)

For people with heart disease or high cholesterol, we recommend getting less than 7 percent of the week's total calories from saturated fat. We also recommend less than 200 milligrams of dietary cholesterol a day.

The chart below lists the maximum number of grams of total fat and saturated fat recommended for your calorie level.

CALORIES PER DAY	TOTAL FAT PER DAY (G)*	SATURATED FAT PER DAY (G)*
1,200	40	12
1,500	50	15
1,800	60	18
2,000	65	20
2,500	80	25

*Your intake should average this much or less over a week.

Note: On average, women consume about 1,800 calories a day and men consume about 2,500.

If you follow these simple recommendations, there isn't a single recipe in this cookbook that you can't fit into your heart-healthy eating plan.

the healthy heart food pyramid

When you're planning a balanced, healthful diet, nothing comes in quite as handy as our Healthy Heart Food Pyramid. As you can see opposite, this pyramid shows at a glance which types of food comprise a heart-smart diet. It also indicates what amounts of the various food groups you should eat.

Experts tell us that the number-one way to get all the nutrients you need is to eat a variety of foods in balanced amounts. That makes sense: Eating only broccoli or only chicken for dinner will limit the nutrients you get. Combine the two and add whole-grain rice, plus our Winter Fruit Compote (page 127) for dessert. Then you'll consume protein, fiber, and a host of vitamins, minerals, and other healthful nutrients.

As you can see from the Healthy Heart Food Pyramid's foundation, the largest part of a help-your-heart diet is made up of breads, cereals, pastas, and starchy vegetables. These bulky, satisfying foods are high in complex carbohydrates and low in fat.

The next-largest section is vegetables and fruits. Packed with fiber, vitamins, and minerals, these foods are virtually fat free.

Near the top of the pyramid, you'll see two food groups. One group, especially high in calcium, contains fat-free milk and nonfat and low-fat dairy products. The other is lean meat, poultry, and seafood, which offer vital protein but contain fat. You should eat less of the foods in these two groups than of the foods in the lower portions of the pyramid.

Finally, at the top of the pyramid, you'll find the foods lowest on the nutritional scale. Because they often contain fats, oils, nuts, and sugars, most desserts fall into this category. That's why you'll want to save such desserts for real celebrations. Nutritious desserts, like many of the ones you'll find in this cookbook, are okay to eat more frequently, however. Some of them, for example, provide a serving of dairy products and/or a serving of fruit.

If your idea of a balanced diet is a doughnut for breakfast, pizza for lunch, and a steak, potatoes, and some pecan pie for dinner, take a closer look at this food pyramid. Just a few changes to your diet can make a big difference in your waistline, your heart health—and your future.

Want to know more about heart health and cooking with your heart in mind? Visit our website at www.americanheart.org.

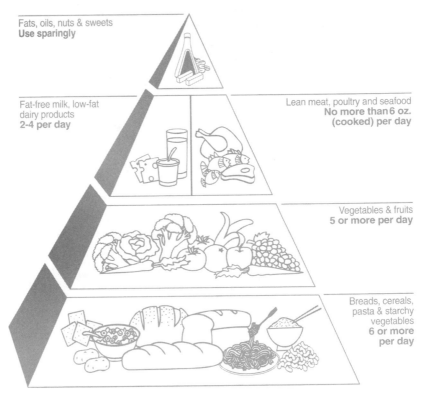

Fats, oils, nuts & sweets
Use sparingly

Fat-free milk, low-fat dairy products
2-4 per day

Lean meat, poultry and seafood
**No more than 6 oz.
(cooked) per day**

Vegetables & fruits
5 or more per day

Breads, cereals, pasta & starchy vegetables
6 or more per day

• The American Heart Association has adapted the Food Guide Pyramid, developed by the U.S. Dept. of Agriculture and U.S. Dept. of Health and Human Services, to be consistent with the AHA Dietary Guidelines for Healthy American Adults.

• Beans and potatoes are included with starchy vegetables.

• Limit your sodium intake to no more than 3,000 milligrams per day.

• Eat no more than 3-4 egg yolks per week. (Egg whites are not limited.)

• For more information, call your local AHA office or 1-800-AHA-USA1 (1-800-242-8721) and ask for the "American Heart Association Diet: An Eating Plan for Healthy Americans" or "Easy Food Tips for Heart-Healthy Eating."

©1994, 1998, American Heart Association

appendix b—
let's talk shopping

Your local supermarket looks safe, but it's actually a major battlefield in the fight against high cholesterol. Why? Because you are what you eat, and you eat what you *buy!* That's why it's important to plan your shopping expedition with your heart in mind—even if you're shopping only for dessert ingredients.

The suggestions we give in How to Adapt Your Favorite Dessert Recipes (pages xvii–xix) can also be very helpful when you shop. The ingredients you'd use to make favorite old recipes more healthful are the ones we recommend using regularly. For instance, when you prepare pie filling that calls for sweetened condensed milk, use the fat-free version. With all the other ingredients in the pie, you really won't notice any difference. The same holds true for a vanilla wafer or graham cracker piecrust. The reduced-fat products make a piecrust that's just as good as the original versions. It's easy to make buying substitutions such as these a routine part of your grocery shopping.

get a clue: read food labels

As a savvy shopper, you know that prepared foods often are loaded with fat, saturated fat, trans fat, cholesterol, sodium, and calories. That's certainly true with many prepared baked goods. Reading nutrition labels can help you find the most nutritious options, whether you're choosing margarine or gingersnaps.

Thanks to the U.S. government, food manufacturers must place a "Nutrition Facts" label on most foods. This label lists the following items per serving:

❖ size

❖ amount of total fat, saturated fat, and cholesterol

❖ number of calories

❖ amount of cholesterol, sodium, and sugars

❖ amount of total carbohydrates, dietary fiber, and protein

❖ amount of vitamins and minerals, expressed as a percentage of your
   daily requirements.

Nutrition Facts

Serving Size ½ cup (114g)
Servings Per Container 4

Amount Per Serving

Calories 90	Calories from Fat 30

	% Daily Value*
Total Fat 3g	5%
Saturated Fat 0g	0%
Cholesterol 0mg	0%
Sodium 300mg	13%
Total Carbohydrate 13g	4%
Dietary Fiber 3g	12%
Sugars 3g	
Protein 3g	

Vitamin A	80%	•	Vitamin C	60%
Calcium	4%	•	Iron	4%

*Percent Daily Values are based on a 2,000 calorie diet. Your daily values may be higher or lower depending on your calorie needs:

	Calories	2,000	2,500
Total Fat	Less than	65g	80g
	Less than	20g	25g
Cholesterol	Less than	300mg	300mg
Sodium	Less than	2,400mg	2,400mg
Total Carbohydrate		300g	375g
		25g	30g

Calories per gram:
Fat 9 • Carbohydrate 4 • Protein 4

When you plan meals, food labels can help you see at a glance how each food fits into your eating plan. They can help you keep track of the amount and kinds of fat, as well as how much cholesterol and sodium and how many calories, you eat.

seeing is believing

The government also requires manufacturers to adhere to strict standards when making claims about their products. When you see, for example, "Fat Free," "Low Fat," or "Lite" on a product, you can be sure what those terms mean. To display certain claims on its package, the food must meet the following criteria:

❖ fat-free — less than 0.5 gram of fat per serving

❖ low-fat — no more than 3 grams of fat per serving

❖ light or lite — one-third fewer calories or no more than half the fat of the regular version; or no more than half the sodium of the regular version

❖ cholesterol-free — less than 2 milligrams of cholesterol and 2 grams or less of saturated fat per serving.

look for the heart-check mark

At the grocery store, you might notice that some food packages bear a heart with a check mark through it. The heart-check mark signifies that the product is part of the Food Certification Program and meets American Heart Association food criteria for saturated fat and cholesterol for healthy people over age two. The heart-check mark is a tool to help you quickly and easily identify foods that can be part of a balanced, heart-healthy eating plan.

American Heart Association

Meets American Heart Association food criteria for saturated fat and cholesterol for healthy people over age 2.

appendix c—
american heart association
operating units and affiliates

For further information about American Heart Association programs and services, call 1-800-AHA-USA1 (1-800-242-8721) or contact us online at http://www.americanheart.org. For information about the American Stroke Association, a division of the American Heart Association, call 1-888-4STROKE (1-888-478-7653).

National Center
American Heart Association
7272 Greenville Avenue
Dallas, TX 75231-4596
214-373-6300

Operating Units of National Center
Office of Public Advocacy
Washington, DC

American Heart Association, Hawaii
Honolulu, HI

Affiliates
Desert/Mountain Affiliate
Arizona, Colorado, New Mexico, Wyoming,
Denver, CO

Florida/Puerto Rico Affiliate
St. Petersburg, FL

Heartland Affiliate
Arkansas, Iowa, Kansas, Missouri, Nebraska, Oklahoma
Topeka, KS

Heritage Affiliate
Connecticut, New Jersey, New York City, Long Island
New York, NY

Mid-Atlantic Affiliate

Maryland, Nation's Capital, North Carolina, South Carolina, Virginia
Glen Allen, VA

Midwest Affiliate

Illinois, Indiana, Michigan
Chicago, IL

New England Affiliate

Maine, Massachusetts, New Hampshire, Rhode Island, Vermont
Framingham, MA

New York State Affiliate

Syracuse, NY

Northland Affiliate

Minnesota, North Dakota, South Dakota, Wisconsin
Minneapolis, MN

Northwest Affiliate

Alaska, Idaho, Montana, Oregon, Washington
Seattle, WA

Ohio Valley Affiliate

Kentucky, Ohio, West Virginia
Columbus, OH

Pennsylvania Delaware Affiliate

Delaware, Pennsylvania
Wormleysburg, PA

Southeast Affiliate

Alabama, Georgia, Louisiana, Mississippi, Tennessee
Marietta, GA

Texas Affiliate

Austin, TX

Western States Affiliate

California, Nevada, Utah
Los Angeles, CA

index